Spanish and Portuguese
16th Century Books

Spanish and Portuguese 16th Century Books
in the
Department of Printing and Graphic Arts

A Description of an Exhibition
and a
Bibliographical Catalogue
of the Collection

Anne Anninger

The Houghton Library
The Harvard College Library · Cambridge, Massachusetts
1985

Funds for the publication of this catalogue have been generously
contributed by
Fundación Juan March, Madrid
Fundação Calouste Gulbenkian, Lisboa
Haven O'More

In Memoriam:
Fernando Zobel de Ayala y Montojo

Foreword

Spanish and Portuguese books hold a special place in the sixteenth-century collections of the Department of Printing and Graphic Arts. Smaller in number than the French or Italian collections, they reflect the rarity of their kind. They are an integral and important part of the cultural record of the Iberian peninsula at the time of its greatest political power, and their graphic quality is of particular distinction, with vivid woodcut images, bold typography, and strong surface design.

Nearly all these Spanish and Portuguese books were collected and given to the Library by the late Philip Hofer, founding Curator of the Department, and they reflect his personal taste and his awareness of the historical importance of such a collection. His interest in this area became focused in 1927, after his first trip to Spain, and in 1931 he acquired his first Spanish book, Enrique Villenas, *Los Trabajos de Hercules*, 1483. This incunabulum was joined by others, but it was the next century in Spain and Portugal on which Mr. Hofer began to concentrate.

He continued to follow his usual practice of collecting, selecting the books one by one, when in 1933, he had the opportunity to acquire fifty-seven Spanish and Portuguese books of the sixteenth century from the James P. R. Lyell collection, five years before the founding of the Department of Printing and Graphic Arts in the Library. The transaction came about through Graham Pollard, at that time associated with the London firm of Birrell and Garnett. Lyell, Scottish-born solicitor, had collected his Spanish books between 1914 and 1927. After their sale, he turned to collecting medieval manuscripts, which he bequeathed to the Bodleian Library. He also endowed the Lyell Readership in Bibliography at Oxford, which Philip Hofer held in 1962, when he was in residence for the Spring term and presented six lectures on The Art of the French Book.

This catalogue is published on the occasion of a special exhibition of Spanish and Portuguese books, composed of forty items, here fully described and illustrated. Following are two hundred and ten bibliographical descriptions, providing a permanent bibliographical record of the collection.

This publication was made possible by a grant from the Fundación Juan March, Madrid, by courtesy of its director Jose Luis Yuste; a grant for the Portuguese section from the Fundação Calouste Gulbenkian, Lisboa, by courtesy of its director José Blanco; and a gift from Haven O'More of Cambridge, Massachusetts, an old friend of the library. We extend our grateful thanks to these supporters, without whose aid the publication of the catalogue would not have been possible.

To our former colleague, Anne Anninger, now Special Collections Librarian at Wellesley College, we owe the catalogue itself. From 1976 to 1982 she was Cataloguer for Printing and Graphic Arts in the Houghton Library, at which time she catalogued the collection. In developing the material into the present exhibition and catalogue she has worked as a tireless volunteer scholar to complete the project.

It is with pride and affection, tempered by sorrow at his death in 1984, that we dedicate this catalogue to the memory of Fernando Zobel de Ayala y Montojo, painter, printmaker, collector, patron, colleague, and Harvard graduate. He played a distinguished and influential role in contemporary Spanish art and culture, and he has a special place in the traditions and the memories of his friends in the Houghton Library.

Eleanor M. Garvey
Philip Hofer Curator of
Printing and Graphic Arts

Preface

As cataloguer for the Department of Printing and Graphic Arts at the Houghton Library, I had the privilege of working with Philip Hofer's acquisitions from 1976 to 1982. Recent purchases of press books, French *livres de fêtes*, and eighteenth-century Venetian imprints passed through my hands. Yet I felt most strongly attracted by the dark beauty of the tooled morocco bindings, the boldness of the typography, and the candor of the woodcuts that I found in the Spanish and Portuguese sixteenth-century collection.

While the French and Italian collections of the period were made widely available by Ruth Mortimer's exemplary catalogues of *French 16th century books* (1964) and *Italian 16th century books* (1974), the Spanish and Portuguese collection remained uncatalogued. With the support of James E. Walsh, Keeper of Printed Books, I set to the task in 1979. Only then did I fully appreciate the depth and quality of Philip Hofer's collecting.

The sixteenth-century Spanish and Portuguese collection provides an overall view of printing and illustration of the time. Far more important, the collection documents the history of printing by region, even by city. It illustrates fine points of stylistic evolution, from the early influx of German type and decorative material and their survival into the 1520s, to the subtle intermingling of native style and Italian influence in the 1530s and 1540s, and Antwerp's increasing domination as the century advances.

Typography and illustration are not the only subjects that the Hofer collection can teach. It also reflects the literary, social and political life of the period. It complements other Harvard collections such as the William Hickling Prescott collection, which the Boston historian built for himself as he researched his *History of the Reign of Ferdinand and Isabella*, published in 1837, and the collection of Luzo-Brazilian material, which John Batterson Stetson Jr. '06 built over many years in memory of his Portuguese stepfather the Count of Santa Eulalia. Prominent among Stetson's gifts is the entire Fernando Palha collection, received in 1928, some 6,700 volumes and pamphlets amassed by the renowned historian to cover the whole field of Portuguese history and literature. Together these collections form a unique resource at Harvard on sixteenth-century Spain and Portugal.

This catalogue of the Hofer collection is in two parts. The forty entries of the exhibition catalogue describe works of particular artistic, literary and historical significance. The two hundred and ten entries of the bibliographical catalogue offer basic descriptions intended for the literary student, historian, bibliographer, collector and rare-book dealer.

The person to whom I had hoped to present my work is no longer with us. Philip Hofer died last November at the age of 86. I am consoled, though, by the thought of our brief encounters in the halls of Houghton, during which I informed him of my progress and let him know how pleased I was to be working on his collection. He would invariably respond that he had taken great pleasure building it. I was particularly touched by his gift, inspired by plans for this exhibition, of additional books for the collection including the rare and magnificent *Compromisso* of 1516.

Second only to Philip Hofer, I want to thank my colleague Roger Stoddard whose unfailing support and thoughtful advice made this catalogue possible. I am most grateful to Sidney Ives who spent many hours editing my text; to Professors Francisco Marquez and Francisco-Joaquim Coelho for their helpful suggestions; to Eleanor Garvey for her help and exemplary patience as I spent many hours working in her department.

To my colleagues at the University Library I owe the receipt, in 1982, of a Douglas W. Bryant fellowship which allowed me to spend three weeks in several Portuguese libraries researching the use of French woodblocks by sixteenth-century Portuguese printers.

To my Houghton colleagues Hugh Amory, Cynthia Naylor, James E. Walsh and Michael Winship go my thanks for their invaluable comments.

Finally I want to thank Eleanor Gustafson, Librarian of the Wellesley College Library, whose generous support and understanding of the demands of such an undertaking allowed me to bring this task to completion.

Anne Anninger
Wellesley College Library

Spanish and Portuguese
16th Century Books

Del primer cielo y del septimo planeta: que es la luna: q̃ tiene enel su assiento

El primer cielo es dõde tiene su assiento la luna: q̃ es el ĩferior planeta:
y seteno: el q̃l esta ꝯstituydo eñl mas
baxo circulo ð la sphera. y en spacio
de ocho años ꝯsuma su circulo: y es
señor ð seteno y vltimo clima. llama se luna q̃si
lucina: porq̃ con ajena lũbre resplãdece: ca toma
la ðl sol: y ministra la en los cuerpos inferiores.
llamarõ la los poetas por tres pricipales efectos
b v

I. Andrés de Li. *Reportorio de los tiempos*. Valencia. Christófol Cofman, 1501.

Spain

I ANDRÉS DE LI. *Reportorio de los tiempos.* Valencia, Christófol Cofman, 1501.

In the prologue, Andrés de Li tells how he decided to enlarge and rewrite a small calendar printed in Saragossa, the *Lunario* of Bernardo de Granollach. The *Reportorio* consists of observations on the seasons, the planets, and the signs of the zodiac, of a calendar with names of Saints and holy days, and of astrological remarks derived from Granollach. Two editions were published in 1495, at Burgos and at Saragossa, of which a number of copies have survived. This, however, is the apparently unique copy of the Valencia, 1501, edition. The printer, Christófol Cofman of Basel, was active in Spain from 1498 to 1517. His edition is particularly interesting for its small woodcut vignettes of undoubted Spanish origin. Skillfully cut, they depict with candor and immediacy the labors of each month, the planets, an anatomical figure with zodiacal indications, and a chilling blood-letting session.

II [LUDOLPHUS DE SAXONIA] *Vita Cristi.* Alcalá de Henares, Stanislao Polono, 1502.

Renowned for their craftmanship, Stanislao "the Pole" and Meinardo Ungut were summoned from Naples to Spain by royal command in 1491. They settled in Seville, using a joint imprint until Ungut's death in 1499. In 1502, Polono was commissioned to start a press at Alcalá de Henares. The *Vita Cristi* was the first book printed in that city. The title-page of its four imposing volumes is illustrated with a woodcut depicting two monks. One of them, probably the translator, Fray Ambrosio Montesino, is presenting the work to Ferdinand and Isabella. Below are the royal arms, which include the emblem of Granada, reconquered by the Catholic kings in 1492. A fitting first for a University city about to become one of the main printing centers of Spain. This copy of volume 4 is printed on vellum.

V. [Giovanni Boccaccio] *Cayda de principles*. Toledo [Pedro Hagembach's successor] 1511.

III *Copilaciõ delos establecimientos dela orden dela caualleria de Sãtiago del Espada.* Sevilla, Juan Pegnicer, 1503.

The constitutions of the Order of Santiago spelled out the spiritual duties and the temporal rules of the Order. This is the revision of 1502 ordered by Ferdinand and Isabella.

The Order of Santiago was founded in the mid twelfth-century, when the Iberian peninsula was divided into six powers: Moslem Spain and the independent Christian kingdoms of Portugal, Leon, Castile, Navarre and Aragon-Catalonia. A group of valiant noblemen, animated by the spirit of the crusades, formed the Order. Knights of Christ, they dedicated themselves to fighting the Infidel. The Order of Santiago played an essential role during the war of the *Reconquista.* As it grew rich in land and in income, so did its political power. Increasingly, the mastership became the object of intrigues by the Crown. In 1476, Isabella petitioned the Pope to grant Ferdinand the administration of the Order. Following the war of Granada (1482-92), in which the Knights fought valiantly, the Pope named the Catholic kings permanent administrators. After three centuries of power and independence, the Order of Santiago was reduced to a mere appendage of the Crown.

A full-page woodcut (on ij^v) depicts Saint James as a victorious knight on horseback, his sword raised high over three fallen Moors.

IV [PEDRO DE ALCALÁ] *Arte para ligeramẽte saber la lẽgua arauiga.* [Granada, Juan Varela de Salamanca, 1504?]

Upon capitulating in 1492, the Moors of Granada were assured that force would not be used to convert them to Christianity. Hernando de Talavera, the trusted confessor of Ferdinand and Isabella, was named the first archbishop of the city and charged with evangelizing its inhabitants. Talavera was a man of integrity and tolerance who with several members of his entourage proceeded to learn Arabic. Relying on persuasion and good example, they made some genuine conversions and earned the respect of the Moors. The Hieronymite father and arabist Pedro de Alcalá was called to Granada to help the archbishop in his endeavour. Alcalá's resulting *Arte* is the first arabic grammar ever published. Its companion volume, the *Vocabulista,* was published in 1505 (see no. 12). Both works were printed by Juan Varela de Salamanca, a printer from Seville who came to Granada in late 1504 at the invitation of the archbishop. The title-page of the *Arte* bears the arms of Hernando de Talavera to whom it is dedicated. A full-page woodcut on the verso depicts the author offering his book to the archbishop.

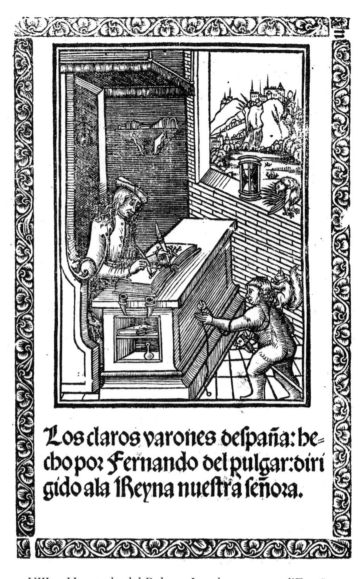

Los claros varones despaña: be=
cho por Fernando del pulgar: diri
gido ala Reyna nuestra señora.

VIII.   Hernando del Pulgar. *Los claros varones d'España.*
[Saragossa, Jorge Coci, ca. 1515]

V [GIOVANNI BOCCACCIO] *Cayda de principes.* Toledo [Pedro Hagembach's successor] 1511.

The *De casibus virorum illustrium* was the first of Boccaccio's works to be rendered into Spanish. Pedro Lopez de Ayala translated the first eight books before his death in 1407, and Alonso de Cartagena, Bishop of Burgos, completed the translation in 1422. Juan Alfonso de Zamora edited their work.

The *Cayda de principes* was first printed in Seville, in 1495. This is the second edition, printed by Pedro Hagembach's anonymous successor active in Toledo from 1503 to 1511. The title-page illustration is after that of the 1495 edition. Depicted are four kings hanging onto a Wheel of Fortune. To the right and on his way up is a king about to reign ("Reinare"); at the top sits a reigning king ("Reino"); to the left, clinging precariously, a third king is on his way down ("Reine"), while at the bottom, hanging upside down, a fourth king has lost his kingdom ("Sin reino so"). A solemn female figure stands on the left. It is *La Fortuna* herself, turning the wheel. The Wheel of Fortune design, used in the last decades of the XVth and throughout the XVIth century, is said to have originated in a XIVth century pavement of the Siena cathedral.

VI BERNARD DE GORDON. *Lilio de medicina.* Toledo, Juan de Villaquirán, 1513.

This is a Spanish translation of Bernard de Gordon's *Lilium medicinae*, one of the most popular medical textbooks of the Middle Ages. Believed to have been a Frenchman, Gordon was educated at Salerno and went on to teach at Montpellier where he composed the *Lilium* in 1303-04. Arabist in content, scholastic in form, it is nevertheless an original work, remarkable for its organization. It is divided into seven particulars, each dealing with a type of disease: fevers, diseases of the head and brain, diseases of vision, respiratory disorders, digestive and other internal diseases, kidney disorders, and diseases of the generative organs. Within each particular, the study of the diseases is subdivided into four sections: causes, symptoms, prognoses and cures. The *Lilium* is the first such book to describe a modern truss, to identify the *petit mal* type of epilepsy, and to mention spectacles ("oculus berellinus").

The first Spanish edition of the *Lilium* was printed in Seville, in 1495. This is the second, and the first book to bear the imprint of Juan de Villaquirán, who began his independent career as a printer in 1512 in Toledo. The Spanish translator is unidentified.

La natura angelica nueuaméte impreſſa:emédada z coꝛregida.

IX.   [Ximénez, Francisco] *La natura angelica*. Burgos, Fadrique de Basilea, 1516.

VII RAMÓN LULL. *Ars inuentiva veritatis.* Valencia, Diego de Gumiel, 1515.

Ramón Lull, scholastic philosopher, mystic and missionary, was born in Palma de Majorca around 1234. He devoted his life to exposing infidel errors, promoting the teaching of Arabic in seminaries, and preaching to the heathens. He composed the *Ars inventiva veritatis* in 1289, in Montpellier. While preaching against Mahommedanism in North Africa, Lull was attacked and stoned, dying of his wounds on June 29, 1315. One of his biographers says it was at Tunis, but most agree Lull was martyred in Bougie, near Algiers. This edition contains a striking woodcut (on C^v) representing Lull at the mercy of the mob. In the background is a city labeled "Bugia." The label, however, is a cancel slip, pasted over the original caption. The uncancelled caption in the British Library copy reads "Tunis."

Formerly in the collection of Ricardo Heredia, this copy bears the Kelmscott House label of William Morris, the Woolley Hall label of George Dunn, and the ex-libris of James P. R. Lyell.

VIII HERNANDO DEL PULGAR. *Los claros varones d'España.* [Saragossa, Jorge Coci, ca. 1515]

Hernando del Pulgar spent most of his life at the Spanish court. He served as page to John II, as secretary to Henry IV and was named chronicler of the kingdom by Ferdinand and Isabella in 1482. He is best known for his *Crónica de los reyes católicos*.

Los claros varones, first published in 1486, is a biographical and anecdotal gallery of notables of the time of Henry IV. It consists of twenty-four biographies including those of the Conde de Haro, the Marqués de Santillana and Cardinal Don Juan de Torquemada. Appended are letters from Pulgar to Queen Isabella and other dignitaries of the period.

This edition is undated and its printer unnamed. His identity, however, is concealed in the woodcut illustration on the title-page: a man is writing at a desk while a child plays with his hobby horse and pet squirrel on a leash. A bookcase sits in the dark corner of the room. Barely discernible, on the left side of the bookcase, is the device of the Saragossan printer Jorge Coci. Coci also used this illustration in his 1513 edition of Vergil's *Opera* and 1518 edition of Petrarch's *De los remedios contra prospera y adversa fortuna*. The *Claros varones* was probably printed around 1515.

de õ Barçelona dõ Ramon depues q̃ ouo hecho muchas coſas
muy ſeñaladas y cõplido hazañas muy glorioſas enſu vida: ſiẽ
do ya muy viejo eſtãdo en Barçelona dio fin a todos ſus traba
jos y partio deſta vida. Donde muriendo en tã vieja edad enel
año del ſeñor. Mbil ciẽto y treynta y vno ſe viſtio el habito õla oz
den de pobres del Hoſpital de Mieruſalẽ enla caſa delos pobres
eneſte habito eſta ſu cuerpo ſepultado enel mõeſterio õ Ripoll.

¶Libro Terçero dela preſente o=
bra trata õ don Ramon Berẽguer
Conde dezeno de Barçelona q̃ fue
principe õ Aragon caſado cõ doña
Petronila hija õ don Ramiro rey
de Aragon donde fue la vnion de=
los dos Principados.

Petronilla Ramon.

Linea delos

Reyes Daragõ.

d·ſãcho cõ õ Roſellõ y Cerdaña.

d·dolca mu ger õl rey õ Portogal.

la muger õ armigol cõ de õ vrgel.

Ornemos pues a don Ramõ Beren=
guer del q̃l arriba començe a hablar:ya
ſea verdad q̃ ſus antepaſſados me han
diuertido y del principal intẽto algo a=
partado. Y pues ami pareçer he conta
do lo q̃ era neçeſſario hablar dellos/ao
ra quiero tornar donde ſali. Caſoſe pu
es (ſegũ començamos a dezir) don Ra
mon Berenguer con doña Petronila
hija de dõ Ramiro el monge rey de A=
ragon:dela qual ouo dos hijos. Doñalonſo aquiẽ dexo el reyno
de Aragõ y el condado de Barçelona. y a don Sãcho q̃ fue con
de de Roſſellon y Cerdaña. ouo otras dos hijas. doña Dolça q̃

XII.   [Lucio Marineo] *Cronica d'Aragon*. Valencia, Joan Joffre, 1524.

IX [XIMÉNEZ, FRANCISCO] *La natura angelica.* Burgos, Fadrique de Basilea, 1516.

La natura angélica is the work of Francisco Ximénez, theologian and social and political writer of fourteenth-century Catalonia. The *Llibre dels angels*, as it is known in Catalan, is a piece of patristic erudition which draws its inspiration from the work of the Pseudo-Areopagite and Saint Bonaventura. Ximénez's stated goal is the propagation of the cult of angels among "simple and devoted persons." *La natura angélica* analyzes the creation, nature, hierarchy and function of angels, and devotes an entire book to the Archangel Saint Michael.

It is not known whether Ximénez wrote the *Llibre dels angels* in Latin or in Catalan. It was first printed in French, however, in 1478, then in Castilian in 1490 and in Catalan in 1494. This is Fadrique Alemán de Basilea's second Castilian edition. Born Friedrich Biel of Basel, Fadrique printed for over thirty years at Burgos. The title-page illustration depicts Saint Michael in armor fighting the devil. Remarkably executed, this block is also innovative as it does away with the traditional relationship of border containing, and illustration contained. The powerful gesture of Saint Michael becomes even more so as his figure — hand and sword, wings, sheath and feet — steps out of the black border of climbing vines.

X JUAN DEL ENCINA. *Cancionero de todas las obras.* Saragossa, Jorge Coci, 1516.

Juan del Encina, poet and musician, was born near Salamanca in 1469. He studied at the University of Salamanca prior to joining the household of the second Duque de Alba in 1492. The same year, he wrote an imitation of Vergil's *Eclogues* and entertained his patron with a dramatic piece entitled *Triunfo de la fama*, which commemorated the conquest of Granada. In 1496 Encina published the *Cancionero*, a collection of poetical works he composed from age fourteen to twenty-five. It contained lyrical pieces as well as eight dramatic eclogues (ten or twelve in later editions). Some of these, performed at Christmas or Easter, during Carnival or Lent, were an echo of medieval liturgical drama. Others, however, were secular in nature, and presented for the first time a group of lay characters, country and market-place people, courtiers, shepherds and students. As such, Encina's *representaciones* marked the transition from the religious to the secular stage and earned him the title of father of Spanish drama.

There were six editions of the *Cancionero* between 1496 and 1512. This is the seventh, printed in 1516 by Jorge Coci. Its title-page is adorned with the woodcut arms of Ferdinand and Isabella.

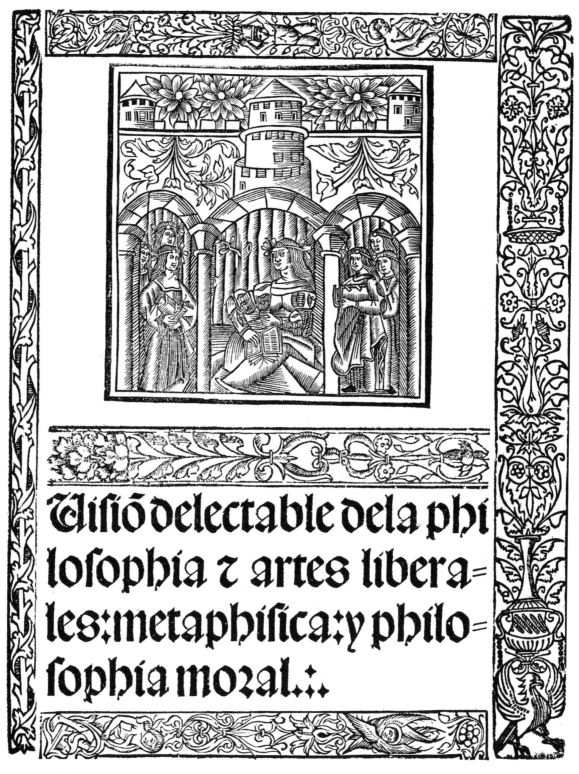

XIV. [Alfonso de la Torre] *Visiõ delectable dela philosophia ⁊ artes liberales.* Sevilla, Jacobo & Juan Cromberger, 1526.

XI LIVIUS. *Las quatorze decadas.* Saragossa, Jorge Coci, 1520.

The *Livy* is one of the most splendid of Jorge Coci's productions. "Alemán de nacion" as his colophons tell us, Coci began his career as apprentice to the Saragossan printer Pablo Hurus. Following his master's death in 1499, Coci formed a short-lived partnership with Leonardo Hutz and Lope Appentegger. By 1504 he was printing alone, making the most of the typographical stock he inherited from Hurus. He was active in Saragossa till his death in 1544. Accurate text, handsome paper, harmoniously laid-out pages and lavish illustrations characterize his production. With Jacobo Cromberger, Jorge Coci is among the best printers of sixteenth-century Spain.

The title-page of the Livy, with its full-page woodcut arms of Charles V, is a remarkable example of four-color printing. More than three hundred woodcuts illustrate the text, some repeated several times. Of German origin, they were cut for Johann Schöffer's *Romische Historie vss Tito Liuio gezogen*, the first German translation of Livy, printed at Mainz in 1505. Coci's mark, an escutcheon hanging from a tree below which two lions lie peaceably, adorns the colophon.

XII [LUCIO MARINEO] *Cronica d'Aragon.* Valencia, Joan Joffre, 1524.

The author of this chronicle of the kings of Aragon was a Sicilian. Educated at Rome, Marineo taught at Palermo before joining the faculty at the University of Salamanca in 1484. He allied himself to the circle of Arias Barbosa and Peter Martyr, and joined with Antonio de Lebrija to restore classical studies in the Peninsula. In 1496 Marineo was summoned to the court of Ferdinand and Isabella. His function was to instruct the members of the household and to improve the Latin of palatine priests. He also acted as historiographer of the king and queen and ended his days as chaplain of the kingdom.

This is the first edition of Juan de Molina's translation of the *Pandit Aragonie veterum primordia regum hoc opus*, originally published in Saragossa in 1509. The arms on the title-page are those of Don Alonso de Aragón to whom the work is dedicated. They are printed in red and black; the green, yellow and brown colors were added by hand in this copy. The illustrations, genealogical trees, and portraits of kings are close copies of those of the 1509 edition and include, on leaf xxiiii^r, the portrait of Raimundus and of his charming fiancée Petronilla.

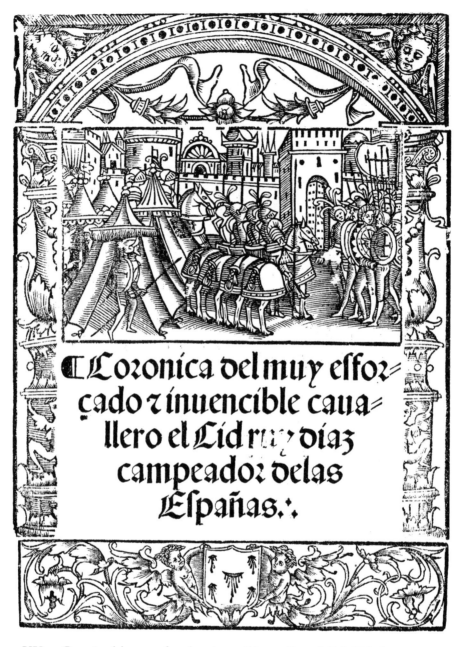

Coronica del muy esforçado z inuencible cauallero el Cid

XV.   *Coronica del muy esforçado z inuencible cauallero el Cid.* Toledo, Miguel
de Eguía, 1526.

14

XIII ROBERTO DE NOLA. *Libro de cozina.* Toledo, Ramon de Petras, 1525.

This is the first Spanish edition of one of the first Spanish cookery books. The *Libro de cozina* was originally published in Catalan, in 1520, by the Barcelona printer Carlos Amorós. Its author is Roberto de Nola, a native of Catalonia and former cook to Ferdinand, King of Naples. In the prologue, Nola relates how the king enjoined him to write his recipes down so that they might be passed on. Nola's cookbook contains recipes for soups, including calf's hoof soup; sauces and dressings, including French mustard; dishes for Lent; broths for invalids, and marzipan and other sweets. It also describes the duties of servants and gives helpful hints for sharpening knives and carving meat and poultry. The title-page is adorned with the arms of Charles V while the recto of the last leaf bears a full-page cut of the arms of Diego Pérez Dávila, alcaide of Logroño, at whose expense the book was published.

XIV [ALFONSO DE LA TORRE] *Visiõ delectable dela philosophia ꝯ artes liberales.* Sevilla, Jacobo & Juan Cromberger, 1526.

The "bachiller" Alfonso de la Torre, a native of Burgos, wrote the *Visión delectable* around 1440 at the request of Juan de Belmonte, tutor of the Prince of Viana. It is an allegorical tale in which Understanding, portrayed as an infant born to an ignorant and sinful world, is instructed by such figures as Grammar, Logic, Rhetoric, Music, Geometry, Arithmetic and Astrology. Truth and her sisters Wisdom, Nature, and Reason complete the education of man with metaphysical disquisitions and moral admonitions. The *Visión* is a remarkable compendium of 15th century knowledge and philosophical reflection, including summaries taken from Maimonides. Of particular interest is a small chapter at the end of the volume entitled "En dónde y por quiẽ fue inuentada la arte de imprimir libros: y en qué año se diuulgó." It dates the invention of printing at 1421, gives Mainz as its birthplace and names the noble and rich citizen Pedro Fuest as its inventor.

The *Visión* is illustrated with a series of woodcut allegorical figures of Spanish origin.

XV *Coronica del muy esforçado ꝯ inuencible cauallero el Cid.* Toledo, Miguel de Eguía, 1526.

There were two *Crónicas del Cid* circulating in print in the early decades of the sixteenth century in Spain. The first was an epic tale drawn from a fourteenth-century manuscript held in the Benedictine monastery of San Pedro de Cardeña. Edited by the abbot Juan de Belorado, it was first printed in Burgos, in 1512, by Fadrique Aleman de Basilea. The second *Crónica* was a popular text, a legend

XV.   *Coronica del muy esforçado z inuencible cauallero el Cid.* Toledo,
Miguel de Eguía, 1526 (f12ʳ).

fashioned by the imagination of generations of tale-tellers and compilers. Subtitled *Suma de las cosas marauillosas que fizo en su vida el buen cauallero Cid Ruy Diaz*, it came out of the Seville press of the *Tres compañeros alemanes* in 1498; it was reprinted at Seville, in 1509. This is the third edition printed by Miguel de Eguía, an excellent craftsman based in Alcalá de Henares, who printed occasionally in Toledo. Two woodcuts illustrate Eguía's *Crónica*. One on the title-page, representing a camp scene in front of a city wall, is contemporary with this edition. The other, showing a skirmish in a city street, is somewhat archaic in style and probably dates back to the fifteenth century.

XVI JUAN DE MENA. *Copilacion de todas las obras.* Sevilla, Juan Varela de Salamanca, 1528.

Juan de Mena was born in Cordoba in 1411. He studied at Salamanca and most probably at Rome. Upon his return to Spain, he was appointed Latin secretary at the court of Castile; he later became chronicler to John II and magistrate in Cordoba. He died in Torrelaguna in 1456. This is the first collected edition of his works. Included is the *Laberinto de Fortuna*, also known as *Las Trescientas* from the number of its *coplas*. The *Laberinto* is an allegorical vision arranged, as in Dante's *Paradiso*, according to the order of the seven planets. The *Coronación* is the author's imaginary journey to Mount Parnassus to witness the coronation, as poet and hero, of his great patron, the Marqués de Santillana. The *Siete pecados mortales*, which deal with the eternal battle between Reason and Will, are here published under the title *Tratado de vicios y virtudes*. Left unfinished, the poem was completed by Gerónimo de Olivares.

This edition is the work of Juan Varela de Salamanca who began his printing career in Seville in 1505, using the types and ornaments of the *Cuatro compañeros alemanes*. Varela went on to print in Granada and Toledo before re-establishing his press in Seville in 1514, where he remained until his retirement in 1538.

XVII [ANTONIO DE GUEVARA] *Libro aureo de Marco Aurelio.* Saragossa, Jorge Coci, 1529.

In 1524, while he lay ill in bed, Charles V asked to read the manuscript of a didactic novel his chronicler, Antonio de Guevara, had been working on for some time. Guevara lent the emperor the text of the *Libro áureo* with the caveat that it not be shown to anyone else. Guevara's admonitions were in vain. The manuscript was stolen and copied. A first pirated edition was published in Seville on February 27, 1528, soon followed by a Lisbon and by a Valencia edition. This is one of three editions of Guevara's pirated text printed in 1529. It consists of forty-eight auto-biographical discourses supposedly written by Marcus Aurelius, together with nineteen "personal" letters from the Roman emperor to intimate acquaintances

XVIII. [Antonio de Aranda] *Verdadera informaciõ d'la Tierra Santa*. Toledo, Juan de Ayala, 1537.

and friends. The *Libro áureo* was an instant success and soon was translated into all European languages. Meanwhile, Guevara reworked his text, incorporating here and there large segments of the *Libro áureo*. His authorized version was published in Valladolid on April 8, 1529, under the title *Relox de príncipes*. A success in its own right, the *Relox* was a novel relating the wise and virtuous life of Marcus Aurelius for the benefit and entertainment of modern sovereigns. As he had done with the *Libro áureo*, Guevara, appealing to an imaginary manuscript in Florence, claimed an historical character for the *Relox*. Modern criticism tends, nevertheless, to consider it as a pure work of fiction.

XVIII [ANTONIO DE ARANDA] *Verdadera informaciõ d'la Tierra Santa.* Toledo, Juan de Ayala, 1537.

The author of the *Verdadera informacion* is Antonio de Aranda, guardian of the Franciscans' convent of Alcalá de Henares and future confessor to the daughters of Charles V. In the dedication to the daughters of the Marqués de Villena, Doña Francisca and Doña Juana Pacheco, Aranda expresses the hope that his travel guide will prompt many Christians to undertake the pilgrimage to the Holy Land. In a first part, the author describes Jerusalem and Judea; in a second, Galilee, Samaria and the "nación de los maronitas;" the last chapter is devoted to the island of Cyprus. Aranda describes and recommends the best routes, places to stay, monuments to visit, and ways to deal with the inhabitants and their idiosyncrasies. To this day his work retains considerable geographical, archaeological and ethnographical interest.

There were two editions at Alcalá de Henares, in 1531 and 1533. This is the third, printed at Toledo by Juan de Ayala. Its title-page depicts the double cross, emblem of the Knights of the Holy Sepulchre. This copy is bound in contemporary black Spanish morocco, blind-tooled in a rope-work pattern and gold-stamped at the center and corners of the covers. The edges are gauffered and gilt.

XIX LUCIO MARINEO. *De las cosas memorables de España.* Alcalá de Henares, Juan de Brócar, 1539.

The *Cosas memorables* is a translation of Lucio Marineo's *De rebus Hispaniae memorabilibus*, first published at Alcalá de Henares in 1530. W. H. Prescott describes it as "a rich repository of details respecting the geography, statistics, and manners of the Peninsula, with a copious historical notice of events in Ferdinand and Isabella's reign." There is a section on the old Spanish tongue, with a list of Basque words and their Spanish equivalents (xxviij^v-xxix^r), and a detailed account of the *reconquista* of Granada in 1492 (Libro XX).

The New World is not omitted. In a paragraph entitled "De otras yslas apartadas del hemispherio llamadas Indias" (clxi^r), Marineo refers to Columbus as "Pedro

XXV. *El septimo libro de Amadis.* Estella, Adrián de Anvers, 1564.

Colon" for the first time on record, but he disputes the claim that Columbus discovered America. According to Marineo, a coin stamped with the effigy of Caesar Augustus was found on American soil and brought back to the Pope, thus proving that the Romans had been acquainted with "*los Indios*" long before the time of Columbus.

XX LUIS DE ALCALÁ. *Tractado d'los prestamos que passan entre mercaderes y tractantes.* Toledo, Juan de Ayala, 1546.

With the economy in a flourishing state, four treatises on commerce were published in the 1540's, each of them an invaluable source for understanding the business practices of the time. Of the four, the *Tractado* is certainly the most old-fashioned in spirit. Its author, Luis de Alcalá, was a Franciscan father. His analysis of the nature of loans, of interest, and of contractual exchanges is bounded by Christian ethics. Of particular concern to him is the struggle between conscience and the desire for profit.

Though they unanimously denounce usury on religious grounds, the other treatises, in particular Saravia de la Calle's *Instrucción de mercaderes muy provechosa*, analyze common practices on commercial grounds. They show signs of the increasing estrangement of religious and economic concerns, and of the overall secularization of culture.

This is the second edition of Alcalá's *Tratado* printed by Juan de Ayala. The title-vignette illustrates one of Saint John Chrysostom's sayings comparing usurious profit to the venom of a serpent; first it numbs, then slowly annihilates the conscience.

XXI VASCO DÍAZ TANCO DE FREJENAL. *Libro intitulado Palinodia.* Orense, Printed by the author, 1547.

Vasco Díaz Tanco, poet, dramatist, translator, indefatiguable traveller and itinerant printer, was born in Fregenal de la Sierra in the late fifteenth century. The biblical plays he wrote as a youth have disappeared; so have thirty of the forty-eight works he lists as his own in the prologue of the *Jardín del alma xp̃iana*. Díaz Tanco printed his own material, probably in a small number of copies, which would explain why so few have survived. Those which have reached us show a great originality in design. The author-printer played freely with his text and his page, making the most of his limited stock of type and woodblocks. The title-page of the *Palinodia* is particularly successful. Above the title printed in red and black is a large portrait of Charles V and Prince Philip on horseback, under the royal arms.

The *Palinodia*, which relates the feats of arms between Charles V and the Turks, is taken for the most part from Paolo Giovio's *Commentario delle cose de Turchi*, and from Andrea Cambini's *Libro della origine de Turchi et imperio delli Ottomani*.

XXVI.   [Olivier de la Marche] *El cavallero determinado*. Barcelona,
Claudio Bornat, 1565.

XXII *La cronica del rey dõ Rodrigo.* Toledo, Juan Ferrer, 1549.

One of the most popular in the genre, the chronicle of Don Rodrigo tells of the fate of the king of the Goths and of the tragic loss of his kingdom to the Moors. The *Crónica* was written in the early fifteenth century and is attributed, on strong evidence, to Pedro del Corral. In the *Generaciones y semblanzas*, Fernán Pérez de Guzmán refers to Corral and his likes as "onbre[s] de poca vergüeña," who spin strange and marvelous tales rather than tell the truth. In Guzmán's words, the *Cronica* is nothing but a "trufa o mentira paladina."

Yet chivalresque escapades and tales such as those of Rodrigo being buried alive and eaten by serpents kept readers enthralled. There were six editions of the *Crónica* between 1511 and 1549. This one is notable for its title-page illustration. While three noblemen beg him to refrain, King Rodrigo orders a servant to open the massive padlocks on the door of the enchanted palace. The sky is heavy with foreboding clouds. The terrible secret is about to be revealed: Rodrigo's reign will soon end in the conquest of Spain by the Moors.

XXIII [PEDRO DE BURGOS] *Libro dela historia y milagros hechos a inuocacion de nuestra Señora de Montserrat.* Barcelona, Pedro Mompezat, 1550.

The author of this work is Pedro de Burgos, abbot of the monastery of Montserrat from 1512 to 1536. This is the second edition (the first came out in 1514) of his colorful description of the sanctuary and of the miracles worked by the famous image of the Virgen de Montserrat, said to have been carved by St. Luke. Within a distinctive outline border of rope-work, the title-vignette depicts the Virgin with the "Monte Serrado" in the background.

Richard Ford refers to his ownership of this copy in his *Handbook of Spain* (1845), mentioning mischievously that it only reports 288 miracles. They increased daily, so that new editions were called for in 1606, 1627 and 1671. Inserted opposite the title-page is the original front fly-leaf inscribed "1551. Got verleich Gluck, T v Freundtsperg . . . Kaufft das Buch zu Monserat im 1551 Jar den 23 Julii umb 3Rl . . . ." On the present front fly-leaf, Richard Ford has added in his own hand ". . . Charles V ascended the mountain 12 July 1551 & Freundtsperg [the commander of Charles V's Hansknechts] bought this copy in the monastery itself."

This is the Heber-Richard Ford-Huth-Lyell copy.

XXVII.   [*Abecedario*] Toledo, Francisco de Guzmán, 1576.

XXIV Gabriel Alonso de Herrera. *Libro de agricultura.*
Valladolid, Francisco Fernández de Cordova, 1563.

Interested in agriculture at an early age, Gabriel Alonso de Herrera gained practical experience on his father's land before going to Granada to further his studies. From 1503 to 1512, Herrera traveled through Spain, Germany, Italy, and France, studying agricultural practices. Upon his return, he wrote the *Obra de agricultura*, which he dedicated to his mentor, Cardinal Cisneros. First published at Alcalá de Henares in 1513, the *Obra* was based on Alonso's readings in classical and medieval texts "de re rustica," and on his own observations. Herrera suspected, for example, the existence of sexes in the botanical realm and could tell apart the male and female flowers of the laurel; he advocated such innovative practices as pruning rather than training branches to obtain larger fruit. His was the first Spanish work to deal in a systematic fashion with such subjects as the quality and properties of the soil, growing and caring for vines, trees, and vegetables, and breeding and tending animals. The *Obra* was published when Spain, at last unified, could concentrate on economic stability and agrarian improvements. The work went through twenty-one editions and several translations before the end of the century.

XXV *El septimo libro de Amadis.* Estella, Adrián de Anvers, 1564.

The *Lisuarte de Grecia* is the seventh book of the *Amadis of Gaul*. A sixteenth-century text, it purports to have been found in London and to be the work of the great magician Alquife, husband of Urganda the fairy. Its authorship has been attributed to Feliciano de Silva. After the mediocre success of the sixth book devoted to Florisando, the adventures of Lisuarte, grandson of Amadis of Gaul, rekindled interest in the series. They began with the disenchanting of the characters left spellbound at the end of the fifth book, and ended with the birth of Lisuarte's son, Amadis of Greece, the future hero of the ninth book.

The *Lisuarte* went through more than ten editions from 1514 to 1584. This is the seventh and probably the rarest of all. Its printer was Adrián de Anvers who, from 1547 to 1567, was active in the small town of Estella in Navarre. The title-page is among his most ambitious: above the title in red, a large woodcut in black shows the hero on horseback. Details such as the footman's headgear, the horse's pompoms, and the impressive array of plumes on Lisuarte's helmet have been overprinted in red.

XXVIII. *La regla y stablescimientos de la cavalleria de Sanctiago del Espada*. Madrid, Francisco Sánchez, 1577. Copy A.

XXVI [OLIVIER DE LA MARCHE] *El cavallero determinado.*
Barcelona,   Claudio Bornat,   1565.

Olivier de La Marche's *Chevalier délibéré*, an allegorical poem celebrating the deeds of Charles le Téméraire, was a favorite of sixteenth-century Europe. Charles V enjoyed it so much that he translated it into Spanish prose which was later versified by Hernando de Acuña. The emperor entrusted his chronicler, Cristóbal Calvete de Estrella, with the privilege and the details of the publication. Calvete paid for and retained the right to the woodcut illustrations by Arnold Nicolaï. He had Jean Steelsius of Antwerp print the *Cavallero* in 1553 in an edition of 2,000 of which a number of copies intended for the Spanish market were lost at sea. Steelsius ran off a second edition in 1555. Upon his return to Spain Calvete petitioned for and obtained a sixteen-year extension for his privilege, "in view of the damage incurred from the loss of seven hundred copies at sea and of the compensation which had to be paid to the merchant selling them." With the Nicolaï blocks he brought back from Antwerp, Calvete had Claudio Bornat of Barcelona print a new edition in 1565, the first edition of the *Cavallero* printed in Spain.

XXVII [*Abecedario*]   Toledo,   Francisco de Guzmán,   1576.

As with anything handled by children, the life span of an ABC is short. All the more remarkable is the freshness of this one, apparently a lone and unrecorded survivor. Its printer, Francisco de Guzmán, was active in Toledo from 1563 to 1578. The block on the title-page is worn, having been used many times before, possibly for earlier editions of this work. While his classmates sit on benches and read, apparently undisturbed, a young lad, pants down and shirt up, is held firmly by an usher while his master scourges him. His *Abecedario* has fallen to the ground. It must contain, like this one and most primers of the time, the ABC, the consonants, vowels and syllables, followed by the Pater Noster, the Ave Maria, Credo and Salve Regina, both in Latin and Spanish. It includes also the beginning of the Ordinary of the Mass, the Introït, Confiteor and Absolution, followed by the ten Commandments and the Catechism. What has the lad done to deserve such punishment? Whatever the case, his pitiful figure serves as a strong admonition to small readers.

XXVIII *La regla y stablescimientos de la cavalleria de Sanctiago del Espada.*
Madrid,   Francisco Sánchez,   1577.

Both Houghton copies of *La regla* are notable for their elaborately tooled contemporary bindings of black morocco. Both have four bands on the back, and edges gilt. The panels of copy A are gold-tooled in concentric borders of rolls and small tools. A wheel or fan with scalloped edges radiates in the center while a three-quarter fan of the same execution decorates each corner of the inner frame.

The panels of copy B are gold-tooled with roll borders of animals and leaves alternating with a border of small tools. Enclosed are two triangular compartments and a rectangular center field with a scallop shell at each corner and a rosette of tools in the center.

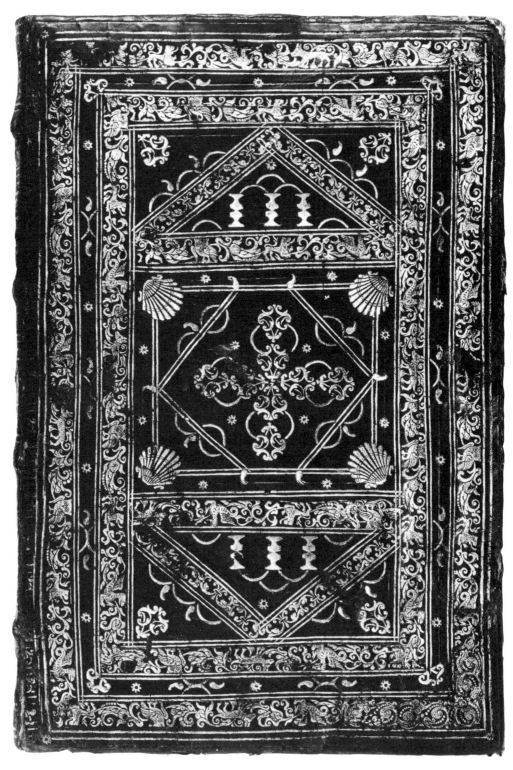

XXVIII. *La regla y stablescimientos de la cavalleria de Sanctiago del Espada.* Madrid, Francisco Sánchez, 1577. Copy B.

XXIX DIEGO DE ÁLABA Y VIAMONT. *El perfeto capitan.*
Madrid, Pedro Madrigal, 1590.

Don Diego de Álaba y Viamont, son of Don Francés, the illustrious *capitán general* of the Spanish artillery, was educated as a humanist and mathematician. He studied Latin and rhetoric with Ambrosio de Morales and Sánchez de las Brozas in Alcalá, and was trained in the exact sciences by Jerónimo Muñoz in Salamanca. Álaba drew upon his father's teachings for the first few chapters of the *Perfeto capitán*, which deal with military discipline. Far more important, however, was his own mathematical contribution to the theory of gunnery. While Leonardo da Vinci's manuscript notes on the flight of projectiles remained unknown to most, Niccolò Tartaglia, in his *Della nova scientia* (1537), was the first to publish investigations of the curve described by projectiles. Álaba's tables, though not yet giving the true range of a projectile, showed great improvement over the principles of his Italian predecessor. Galileo would be the first to take fully into account the resistance of air in calculating the trajectory and range of a projectile.

Portugal

XXX *Liuro ꝛ legẽda que fala de todolos feytos ꝛ payxoões dos sãtos martires.* Lisbon, João Pedro Bonhomini de Cremona, 1513.

The *Legenda*, best known as the *Flos Sanctorum*, is a compilation of the lives of the Saints and of the life and Passion of Christ. According to the prologue, it is the work of the Reverend Father Gaubert and is derived in part from Jean Gerson's *Monotheseron*. The *Legenda* was translated from Latin into Spanish at the end of the 15th century. It is here published in Portuguese for the first time, at the express command of King Dom Manuel. The King, renowned for his missionary fervor, was in the habit of dispatching theologians and books of Christian doctrine to far lands. Among the books taken to the Negus by Duarte Galvão's embassy to Abyssinia in 1515 were "cem liuros da vida e paixã dos marteres, ẽcadernados de tauoas, meos cubertos de coiro." Most probably these were copies of this very edition of the *Legenda*, which Bonhomini de Cremona had printed eighteen months earlier for Dom Manuel.

XXXII. *O compromisso da Confraria de Misericordia.* Lisbon, Valentim Fernandes & Hermão de Campos, 1516.

¶ Do compromisso τ regimento dos officiaes da sancta confraria de Mi sericordia.

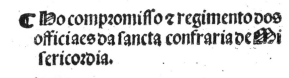

Om Manuel per gra ça de os Rey de Portu gal τ dos alguarues da quem τ daalem mar em affrica Senhor de guy nee τ da conquista. naue gaçam τ comercio de E thiopia. Arabia. Per sya τ da India. ¶A quantos esta nossa carta virem: fa zemos saber. que pollo proueador τ officiaes da confra ria da Misericordia desta muy nobre τ sempre leal çida de de Lyxboa. nos foy apresentado huu compromisso que pera bõa gouernança da dita cófraria per elles era feito de que ho trelado de verbo a verbo he o q se segue.

¶Prologo.

Eterno immenso τ todo podero so senhor os. padre das miseri cordias: começo meo τ fim de to da bondade. açeytando as prezes τ rogos de alguus justos τ temé tes a elle. quis repartir có os pe cadores parte da sua misericor dia. E em estes deradeiros dias inspirou nos coraçóes de alguus boós τ fiees xpãaos. τ lhe deu coraçam: siso: forças τ caridade: pera ordenaré hua jrmandade τ con fraria. sob titulo τ nome τ emvocaçam de nossa senho ra a madre de os virgem Maria da Misericordia. pella

a

¶ O circulo grande reprefenta a equinocial τ o feu centro ao polo do norte. As linhas dereitas fam os rumos δ norteful: τ as outras duas linhas curuas de bũa parte τ da outra fam nordefte fuduefte τ noroefte fuefte. E as outras antre eftas τ a equinocial fam les nordefte oes fuduefte: τ oes noroefte les fuefte.

XXXIII.   Pedro Nunes. *Tratado da sphera*. Lisbon, Germão Galharde, 1537.

XXXI *Liuro primeiro [-quinto] das ordenações.* Lisbon, João Pedro Bonhomini de Cremona, 1514.

One of Dom Manuel's first acts upon acceding to the throne was to order a revision of the statutes inherited from his predecessors. Members of his council set to the task, issuing in 1512-1513 the first two books of the *Ordenações*. In 1514 these were superseded by the five books of *Ordenações* printed by João Pedro Bonhomini de Cremona. Bonhomini completed books 3, 4 and 5 between March and June, reprinting books 1 and 2 in October and December. The title-pages of books 3 and 4 bear the arms of João II, from an old block used by Valentim Fernandes in his 1495 edition of *Vita Christi*. By June of 1514, Bonhomini had commissioned two new blocks for the *Ordenações*: the arms of Dom Manuel with the griffin at the top, and Dom Manuel's sphere with the legend *Spera in Deo et fac bonitatem*. According to the chroniclers, this device was given to Dom Manuel as a young boy by his cousin the King Dom João II. The 1514 edition of the *Ordenações* was ordered destroyed in March of 1521, following the publication of a new edition by Jacobo Cromberger. Only a handful of copies have survived.

XXXII *O compromisso da Confraria de Misericordia.* Lisbon, Valentim Fernandes & Hermão de Campos, 1516.

Devoted to the care of the sick and the homeless, to visiting prisoners and burying the dead, the Confraria de Misericordia was instituted in Lisbon in August 1498 by Dona Leonor, then regent of the kingdom. Hermão de Campos and Valentim Fernandes first printed the rules of the brotherhood in 1516. Apparently only three copies of this edition have survived, one in the Santa Casa de Misericordia of Évora Monte, one in the Museu de Arte Sacra of Lisbon and this one. To the confusion of bibliographers, Germão Galharde issued a close reprint of the *Compromisso* around 1548, copying the layout and the colophon, and using some of the blocks of the 1516 edition. The borders of fruit, flowers and birds which surround Galharde's title-page, however, are the giveaway. Of French origin, they were cut for Geofroy Tory's quarto edition of the *Hore*, printed in Paris in 1527, by Simon du Bois. Luiz Rodrigues purchased them and brought them to Portugal in 1539. He used these borders in at least six of his editions (see also nos. XXXVI, 188 and 191) and lent or sold them to Germão Galharde (see no. 189). They appear in the stock of Portuguese printers throughout the 16th century.

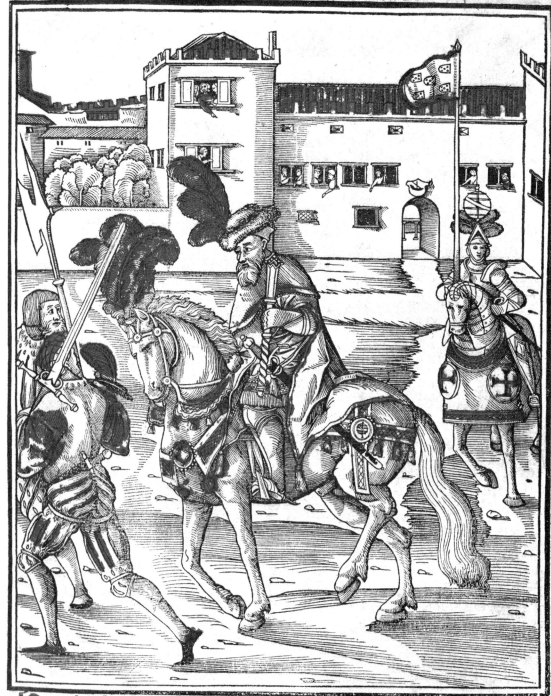

Verdadera informaçam das terras do Preste

Joam/segundo vio z escreue o ho padre Francisco Aluarez capellã del Rey nosso senhor. Agora nouaméte impresso por mandado do dito senhor em casa de Luis Rodriguez liureiro de sua alteza.

XXXV.   Francisco Alvares. *Ho Preste Joam das Indias*. [Lisbon] Luiz Rodrigues, 1540.

XXXIII PEDRO NUNES. *Tratado da sphera.* Lisbon, Germão Galharde, 1537.

More than any others, the Portuguese cosmographers and navigators of the Renaissance put the geographical and astronomical theories of the ancients to the test of empirical observation. The work of the royal cosmographer Pedro Nunes exemplifies this interplay of theoretical knowledge and experience. In the *Tratado*, he offers a translation of Sacro Bosco's *Sphaera*, of Peurbach's *Theorica do sol & da lua* and of the first book of Ptolemy's *Geographia*, "for they contain principles which any person versant in cosmography must know." Then follow Nunes's own reflections prompted by the difficulties Martim Affonso de Sousa experienced while sailing back from Brazil in 1533. Nunes attributes Sousa's troubles to cartographical errors. He distinguishes between navigation by the great circle or orthodromic method, in which the course of a ship crosses successive meridians at variable angles; and navigation by the fixed course or loxodromic method, in which the crossing angle remains constant. Nunes describes the loxodromic curve, pointing the way for Mercator and the Flemish navigators.

XXXIV *Capitolos de cortes.* Lisbon, Germão Galharde, 1539.

These are the petitions issued by the *Cortes* held in Torres Novas in 1525, and in Evora in 1535. They are followed by João III's answers and by the thirty-six laws he promulgated as a result of the *Cortes*, on November 29, 1538. *Capitolos, repostas* and *leyes* speak vividly of the social concerns of the time, of the undesirable presence of gypsies in the kingdom, of the shameful begging on the part of cripples who could otherwise support themselves, and of hungry trustees who despoil orphans of their estate.

This copy is printed on vellum and bound in contemporary blind-tooled calf.

XXXV FRANCISCO ALVARES. *Ho Preste Joam das Indias.* [Lisbon] Luiz Rodrigues, 1540.

The half mythical figure of Prester John, the Christian prince of the East, long haunted the dreams of Portuguese navigators. An envoy of Dom João II, Pedro de Covilham, reached the Abyssinian emperor in 1487, but was never allowed to return to Portugal. A second Portuguese mission, with Duarte Galvão as ambassador and Frai Francisco Alvares as one of its members, set out for Abyssinia in 1515. Delayed by Galvão's death, the envoys reached the court of Prester John in 1521. There they remained for six years, during which Alvares recorded their adventure, describing in great detail the romantic figure of the emperor, his faraway land, its inhabitants, and their curious mores. Published in 1540, Alvares's *Verdadera informaçam* was instantly popular and was soon translated into Italian, French, Spanish, and German.

L. ANDREAE
RESENDII
De uerborũ coniu-
gatione commen-
tarius.
OLISIPONE
Apud Lodouicũ
Rhotorigium ty-
pographum.

XXXVI.   André de Resende. *De uerborũ coniugatione commentarius*. Lisbon,
Luiz Rodrigues, 1540.

XXXVI ANDRÉ DE RESENDE. *De uerborũ coniugatione commentarius.* Lisbon, Luiz Rodrigues, 1540.

André de Resende spent many years abroad studying Latin, Greek, and Hebrew with Antonio de Lebrija, Arias Barbosa and Nicolas Clénard. Upon his return to Portugal in 1540, he became tutor of the Infante Dom Duarte. The same year he published this conjugation manual for Dom Miguel de Menezes, 3rd count of Alcoutim, and for his sister Dona Juliana. Resende's main interest, however, lay in his archaeological studies. Barbosa Machado tells us that Resende carried these "to such an excess, that he never went anywhere without tools to extract [Roman antiquities] from the entrails of the earth." Publication of the *Historia da antiguidade da cidade de Evora* in 1553, and the *De Antiquitatibus Lusitaniae* in 1593, earned him the title of "father of archaeology" in Portugal.

Luiz Rodrigues's title-page is particularly graceful. The small architectural frame containing the title is surrounded in turn by a compartment border of fruit, flowers, and birds cut originally for Geofroy Tory's quarto edition of the *Hore*, Paris, 1527 (see above no. XXXII).

XXXVII [DIEGO DE SAGREDO] *Medidas d'l romano.* Lisbon, Luiz Rodrigues, 1542.

Little is known of Diego de Sagredo other than his Spanish origin and his long residence in Rome. There he was inspired to transmit his knowledge of the new architecture to his fellow countrymen. His *Medidas* was first printed in Toledo in 1526. It was published in French in an elegant edition by Simon de Colines in 1539, and again in Lisbon in 1541. Sagredo's work filled a void. Renaissance architects were surrounded by vestiges of antiquity, they studied the ideals of classical architecture, but they lacked a work of practical interpretation. Sagredo's *Medidas* served just that purpose. It dealt with the detail of antique architecture, the measure and proportion of columns, capitals and bases, arches and porticos. It applied the concepts enunciated by Vitruvius Pollio to modern needs.

Don Florando.

¶Comiença la coronica del valiente y esforçado príncipe dõ Florãdo ð Inglatierra
hijo ðl noble yesforçado príncipe Paladiano
en q̃ se cuentã las grãdes y marauillosas auẽ
turas a q̃ dio fin por amores ðla hermosa prí
cesa Roselinda hija del empador de Roma.

XXXIX. *La coronica del valiente y esforçado príncipe dõ Florãdo d'Inglatierra.* Lisbon, Germão Galharde, 1545.

XXXVIII JERONYMO OSORIO. *De nobilitate civili, de nobilitate christiana.* Lisbon, Luiz Rodrigues, 1542.

Jeronymo Osorio's first published work was written at age thirty, in 1536, while he was studying theology and Hebrew in Bologna. Though he considered himself "adolescens" at the time, Osorio exhibits already in the *De nobilitate* the mature traits which earned him the title of "Cicero portugues": a clear, simple style, at its best when fired by polemic. The work denounces both the ideas of the Stoics and of Machiavelli. Stoicism, according to Osorio, does not bring inner peace but stupor as it stunts the soul's natural aspiration to grandeur. Paradoxically, Machiavelli, "impurus quidam scriptor atque nefarius," attacks Christianity on rather similar grounds. According to him, Christianity destroys heroism by extolling humility and modesty as virtues. Humility, retorts Osorio, does not exclude magnitude. The great heroism of Christian martyrs suffices to expose the fallacy of Machiavelli's theories.

XXXIX *La coronica del valiente y esforçado prīcipe dõ Florãdo d'Inglatierra.* Lisbon, Germão Galharde, 1545.

Although written in Spanish, *Florando da Inglaterra* is a Portuguese addition to romance literature. Its author is a native of Lisbon who professes to have translated the work from English while residing on business in the "noble and . . . celebrated isle of England." He apologizes for errors as "it was difficult to translate such a barbarous language as English," and dedicates his labor to the knights, matrons and maidens of Lisbon. The plot tells of the great and marvelous adventures that the valiant and mighty prince Florando accomplished for love of the beautiful Princess Rosalinda, daughter of the Emperor of Rome. This romance was never reprinted in the Peninsula. The first part, which deals solely with Florando's father Paladiano, was translated by Claude Colet as *L'Histoire Palladienne* (Paris, 1555). This French version was translated in turn by Anthony Munday as *The famous pleasant, and variable Historie of Palladine of England* (London, 1588). One of the handsomest works from the press of Germão Galharde, the *Florando* is illustrated with over one hundred cuts depicting scenes of chivalry.

XL. *Coronica do condeestabre d' Portugall Dom Nuno Aluarez Pereyra.* Lisbon, Germão Galharde, 1554.

40

XL *Coronica do condeestabre d' Portugall Dom Nuno Aluarez Pereyra.* Lisbon, Germão Galharde, 1554.

This is the biography of Portugal's national hero, the "Holy Constable" Nuno Álvares Pereira (1360-1431). His name is synonymous with Portugal's heroic struggle for independence. It speaks of Aljubarrota and of João I's accession to the throne, of the victory of Valverde, and of the final defeat of the Castilians. His secular mission accomplished, Nun' Álvares devoted himself to the Lord's service, retiring to the convent of Sancta Maria do Carmo in Lisbon. Several authorities have attributed the authorship of this work to Fernão Lopes (1380-1449), chief chronicler of the kingdom. This doubtful attribution rests mainly on the inclusion of chapters of the *Coronica* in Lopes's chronicles of Dom Fernando and Dom João I.

This second edition of the *Coronica* is notable for its two woodcut portraits, a form of illustration seldom found in works of the period. The full figure of the Constable, clad in armor on the verso of the title-page is from the block used in Galharde's first edition (Lisbon, 1526). The bust portrait of Nun' Álvares in the habit of a Carmelite was cut for this edition.

Bibliography

The 210 entries of the bibliographical section of this catalogue describe the six-teenth-century Spanish and Portuguese holdings of the Department of Printing and Graphic Arts at the Houghton Library. Fully catalogued, these items are accessible through the Houghton and Widener card catalogues.

The bibliography is arranged in two chronological sequences numbered continuously, one for the Spanish, the other for the Portuguese books. Within each sequence, entries are arranged by year, month, and day. Books dated only by year follow the fully dated entries for the year. Works published over a period of years are entered at the date of the concluding volume. Falsely dated works are entered under their real or ascribed date of publication. A question mark following a supplied date indicates an approximate range of two years, while a "ca." preceding a supplied date indicates an approximate range of five years before or after the date. Justification for supplied dates is given in a note. For example: 1520, 1505-1520, 1517 [i.e. 1520], 1520?, ca. 1520. Where two or more entries fall under a date identical in form, they are arranged alphabetically by heading.

Each entry is composed of a heading incorporating the entry number and the year-date. If supplied, the year-date is bracketed. Headings, including personal names and form headings, conform to those in the Harvard card catalogues. An author's name which does not appear on the title-page is bracketed. If it is found within the book, there is a note to that effect. Titles are literal transcriptions of spelling and punctuation. Capitalization is governed by cataloguing rules. Omitted words are indicated by the customary three points. Imprints in the vernacular are normalized and shortened (place, printer or publisher, date). Latin imprints are given in English, normalized and shortened. When taken from the colophon, imprint information is given in square brackets following the word "Colophon:". When supplied, imprint information is bracketed and justified in a note.

The collation line consists of a format statement followed by the signature collation, which includes, in parentheses, the location of plates integral to the sheets. The paginary collation is given by pages or leaves as the case may be, bracketed if unnumbered, and with indication of the location of blanks. Faulty numbering is accounted for in the collation itself or in a note when the error is sustained. Plates are given as "leaves of plates" at the end of the paginary collation, following a comma when they are integral with the sheets; following a double blank space when they are not integral with the sheets. The measurement of the book is given in centimeters to the nearest half-centimeter, and the number of copies is given if there is more than one.

Notes may explain attributions to authors or printers, localization of printing or dating. Notes may also include an illustration statement tracing the transmission or imitation of woodblocks from one printer to another; an edition or translation note; an imperfect note; a binding note for contemporary bindings other than plain vellum, and an ex-libris statement arranged in order of provenance.

References list in alphabetical order the bibliographies and works of reference that cite the book in question. Often cited references are given in shortened form whereas single citations of books and articles are given in full. Reproductions are mentioned with the abbreviation "fig."; substantial variations from the copy at hand are indicated in parentheses; imperfect copies are noted with the abbreviation "(impf.)". A complete list of the references given in shortened form can be found at the end of the catalogue.

The three indices at the end of the volume incorporate both the exhibition and the bibliography section of this catalogue. The Index of Authors and Titles lists alphabetically and in a single sequence the names of known or ascribed authors and the titles of anonymous works or of works whose author is not named on the title-page. The Index of Cities and Printers is arranged alphabetically by city. Listed under each city are the names of the printers in alphabetical order. The works of each printer are arranged in chronological order under his name. When a printer is active in more than one city, the note "also active in . . ." refers to his work in other location(s). A work ascribed to a printer is preceded by an asterisk. Unassigned works are grouped chronologically under the heading "Unassigned" at the end of the listing for a given city. Rarely signed, woodblocks of the period occasionally bear initials or a monogram. The Index of Illustrators lists such initials alphabetically, followed by the full name of the illustrator in parentheses when he has been identified.

Though they depict some of the finest examples of the collection, the twenty photographs illustrating this catalogue cannot do justice to the originality and the range of design and typography that characterize these Spanish and Portuguese books. They are offered as inducements for the reader to look at the books themselves.

Spain

1. 1501 PALENCIA, SPAIN (DIOCESE)

Cõsticioẽs τ estatutos hechos τ ordẽados por el muy reuerẽdo y magnifico señor dõ fray Diego de Deça obispo d' Palencia . . . [Colophon: Salamanca, 13 de febrero 1501].

Collation: f°. π⁸, a-d⁶, e⁸, f-i⁶, l⁴, m-n⁶, o¹⁰; [90] leaves (leaves [64] and [90] blank). 27cm.

Attributed to the press of Juan de Porras. — Cf. Norton 456. Ex-libris of James P. R. Lyell.

Ref: Lyell p. 76 and fig. 57; Norton 456 (o2-5 missigned oj-iiij); Palau 71529; Vindel, Man. 792.

2. 1501 LI, ANDRÉS DE.

Reportorio de los tiempos. [Colophon: Valencia, Christófol Cofman, 17 de diciembre 1501].

Collation: 4°. a-h⁸, i⁴; [68] leaves. 21cm.

Apparently a unique copy; the illustrations are probably from the blocks used in Pablo Hurus' Saragossa, 1495 edition. — Cf. Martin Kurz. *Handbuch der Iberischen Bilddrucke des XV. Jahrhunderts.* Leipzig, 1931, no. 39. Full contemporary vellum portfolio with overlap and strap.

Ref: Norton 1155.

3. 1502 [LUDOLPHUS DE SAXONIA]

Vita cristi cartuxano romãçado por fray Ambrosio. [Colophon: Alcalá de Henares, Stanislao Polono, 24 de diciembre de 1502].

Collation: f°. A⁸, Aa-Zz⁸, AA-SS⁸, TT⁶; [8], clx, clviij-clxxvj, clxxviij-cccxvij, cccxvj-cccxxix, [1] leaves (last leaf, blank, wanting). 30.5cm.

Author named in colophon. Constitutes v.4 of the *Vita cristi.* Printed on vellum. Full contemporary black morocco, repaired. The Rahir copy.

Ref: BM; Catalina 1; Fernández 1; Heredia 67 and fig.; Lyell p. 68 and fig. 53; Norton 1; Palau 131075;

Aloys Ruppel. *Stanislaus Polonus.* Kraków, 1970, no. 100 and fig.; Salvá 3435.

4. 1503 [EYMERICUS, NICOLAUS]

Directorium inquistorũ. Sequuntur decretales tituli de summa trinitate et fide catholica. [Colophon: Barcelona, Joan Luschner, 28 September 1503].

Collation: f°. a-i⁸, k-n¹², o-z⁸, τ⁸, ɔ⁸, ⁊⁸, χ⁸; [232] leaves. 31cm.

Author named on [224]ᵛ. Leaf [225] misbound after leaf [231]. Ex-libris of James P. R. Lyell.

Ref: B. Col. III, p. 47; BM; Gallardo 2157; Lyell p. 56 and fig. 43 (mentions a copy printed on vellum); Norton 149; Palau 20870

5. 1503 ORDEN MILITAR DE SANTIAGO.

Copilaciõ delos establecimientos dela orden dela cauallería de sãtiago del espada. [Colophon: Sevilla, Juan Pegnicer, 4 de noviembre 1503].

Collation: f°. π², st⁴, a⁶, b-g⁸, h⁶, i⁴, τ⁴, A-B⁸, C¹⁰, D-N⁸, O¹⁰; [6], ij-viij, x-lxv, [5], cxvj leaves. 29cm.

Edited by Juan Fernández de la Gama. π2 misbound after st4; margins of O9, 10 repaired. Ex-libris of the Duque de Hijar.

Ref: BM; Escudero 132; Heredia 2956; Norton 729; NUC; Palau 61510; Salvá 1641 (note); Vindel, Man. 690a.

6. [CA. 1503] [ERLA, JAUME DE]

Doctrina coz los pares deuen criar los fils axi al seruey de deu: coz ha honor del mon. [Barcelona, ca. 1503].

Collation: 4°. a-c⁸; [24] leaves (last leaf, presumably blank, wanting) 18.5cm.

Author named on [2]ʳ. Attributed to the Barcelonian press of Nicolaus Spindeler. — Cf. Norton 89.

Ref: Palau 80546 ([Valencia, Nicolaus Spindeler, 1498]); Vindel, Arte, III, 78 ([Valencia, 1498]).

7.   1504   CATALONIA. LAWS, STATUTES, ETC.

Constitucions. [Colophon: Barcelona, Gabriel Pou, 7 de febrer 1504].

Collation: f°. [-⁸]; [8] leaves (last leaf, presumably blank, wanting). 32cm.
Ex-libris of James P. R. Lyell.

Ref: Aguiló 1297; Lyell p. 60 and fig. 45-46; Norton 162; Palau 60367; Vindel, Man. 670.

8.   1504   LULL, RÁMON.

Apostrophe: Raymundi. [Colophon: Barcelona, Pere Posa, 14 August 1504].

Collation: f°. A-B⁶; xi, [1] leaves (last leaf, blank, wanting). 28cm.

Ref: BM; HS; Norton 92; Palau 143779; Rogent & Durán 32.

9.   1504   [DURAND, GUILLAUME, BP. OF MENDE]

Rationale diuinoↄ officioↄ. [Colophon: Granada, Juan Varela de Salamanca, 12 December 1504].

Collation: f°. A⁴, a-z⁸, ⱬ⁸, ↄ⁸, ↄ⁸, A-G⁸, H¹⁰; [4], cclxxiiij leaves. 30cm.

Author named on [2]ʳ. Ex-libris of James P. R. Lyell.

Ref: BM; Burger p. 74; Lyell p. 248 and fig. 195-97; Norton 347; NUC; Palau 77569 (impf.).

10.   [1504?]   ALCALÁ, PEDRO DE]

Arte para ligeramẽte saber la lẽgua arauiga. [Granada, 1504?]

Collation: 4°. a-f⁸; [48] leaves. 21cm.

Printed by Juan Varela de Salamanca; the woodcut illus. on t.-p. (ecclesiastical arms of Hernando de Talavera, archbishop of Granada) is from the block used in Varela's 1504 edition of Guillaume Durand's Rationale divinorum officiorum (see no. 9).

Ref: BM (Arte and Vocabulista (no. 12) catalogued as 2 pts.); Gallardo 87; Heredia 1485; Norton 348 (before 5 Feb. 1505); NUC (facsimile of the HS copy); Palau 5697; Salvá 2189.

11.   1505   JOANNES CLIMACUS, SAINT.

Scala spiritualis sācti Joannis Climaci. [Colophon: Toledo, 3 January 1505].

Collation: 4°. A⁴, a-s⁸, t⁶; [4], CL leaves. 22cm.

Ascribed to the press of Pedro Hagembach's successor. — Cf. Norton 1042. In this copy, line 5 of colophon on CLʳ reads " . . .Toletana / i sui Reuerēdissimi . . . "; as described in Norton 1042, it reads " . . .Toletana / iussu Reuerēdissimi . . . ". For a discussion concerning the woodcut illus. on t.-p. (St. Ildefonso receiving the chasuble at the hands of the Virgin) see Lyell p. 90 and Lyell, Ximenes p. 56. Translated from the Greek by Ambrosius Camaldulensis Traversarius. Ex-libris of James P. R. Lyell.

Ref: BM (printed on vellum); Palau 292613; Pérez Pastor, Toledo 35.

12.   1505   [ALCALÁ, PEDRO DE]

Vocabulista arauigo en letra castellana. [Colophon: Granada, Juan Varela de Salamanca, 5 de febrero 1505].

Collation: 4°. a-z⁸, A-K⁸, L⁶; [270] leaves. 20cm.

Author named in colophon. The woodcut illus. on both sides of t.-p. are from the blocks used in Alcalá's Arte para ligeramente saber la lengua araviga, [Granada, 1504?] (see no. 10).

Ref: BM; Gallardo 89; Heredia 1486; HS; Norton 349; NUC (facsim. of the HS copy); Palau 5697; Salvá 2191.

13.   1505   LIVIUS. SPANISH. LÓPEZ DE AYALA.

Las decadas de tito liujo. [Colophon: Burgos, Andres de Burgos, 24 de mayo 1505].

Collation: f°. a-z⁸, ⱬ⁶, ↄ⁶, ↄ⁶, A⁴; cxcvi, [10] leaves. 29.5cm.

The woodcut illus. on t.-p. (knight kneeling before king) is from the block used in Juan de Burgos' edition of Alfonso de Cartagena's Doctrinal de los caballeros, Burgos, 1497. Translated by Pedro López de Ayala. Ex-libris of James P. R. Lyell.

Ref: HS; Lyell p. 198-99 and fig. 156; Norton 314; Palau 139126.

14. 1505 MARQUILLES, JAIME.

Comentaria Jacobi de Marquilles super vsaticis bar-chiñ. [Colophon: Barcelona, Joan Luschner, 7 September 1505].

Collation: f°. π⁴, a-z⁸, τ⁸, ɔ⁸, ℞⁸, aa-ff⁸, gg⁴, A-Q⁸, R¹⁰; [4], cccxcviii leaves. 28cm.

Printed on vellum with the exception of signatures A and B (leaves cclxi-lxxvi), which are printed on paper. Ex-libris of Ricardo Heredia.

Ref: BM (paper); HS; Heredia 296; Norton 156; NUC (paper); Palau 152815.

15. 1506 PEREZ DE VALENCIA, JAIME.
COMMENTUM IN PSALMOS.

[Begins [a]1ʳ:] Reuerendi et optimi patris d'o iacobi d' valentia . . . in libros psalmorum dauid prefatio. [Colophon: Barcelona, Nicolaus Spindeler, 31 August 1506].

Collation: f°. a-b⁸, c⁶, a-z⁸, A-I⁸, L-O⁸, P¹⁰, χ⁸; [23, the first blank], cccxxxii (i.e. 296), [9, the first and last blank] leaves (last leaf wanting). 30cm.

Numerous errors in foliation. The full-page wood-cut illus. on leaf [23]ᵛ (David kneeling, with army, castle and ship in background) is from the block used in Spindeler's 1499, Valencia edition of Narcís Vin-yoles' *Omelia sobre lo psalm del Miserere*; some pieces of the border belonged originally to the Barcelonian printer Joan Luschner. Ex-libris of James P. R. Lyell.

Ref: HS (impf.); Lyell p. 24 and fig. 16; Madurell & Rubió p. 390; Méndez-Hidalgo p. 58; Norton 88; Palau 22616, ii.

16. 1506-07 TOSTADO, ALONSO.

Tostado sobre el eusebio . . . [Colophons: Salaman-ca, Hans Gysser, 28 de setiembre, 9 de febrero, 13 de marzo 1507].

Collation: f°. Parts 1, 3, and 4 only of 7pts., in 2v. 31.5cm.
Pt.1: a⁴, a-y⁸, z⁶; [4], clxxxij leaves.
Pt.3: a⁴, aa-qq⁸, rr¹⁰; [4], cxxxviij leaves.
Pt.4: a⁶, AA-YY⁸; [6], clxxvj leaves.

Each pt. preceded by a full-page woodcut and an index, separately signed; pts. 3-4 have caption titles only. Ex-libris of the Livraria de Palha in v.1.

Ref: BM; Burger p. 41; Haebler, Early printers p. 144 (pts. 1-5 only); Heredia 77; HS (2 copies of pts. 1-2); Norton 549; NUC; Palau 146759-66;

Palha 2379 (pt. 1 only); Salvá 4021; Vindel, Man. 3001 (pts. 1-5 only).

17. 1508 CATHOLIC CHURCH. POPE, 1503-1513 (JULIUS II)

Indulgencia del hospital de señor Santiago: nueua-mente concedida por el papa Julio . . . [Santiago?] 1508.

broadside 31.5 × 22cm.

Printed on paper and filled out in ms. to la "marq'sa doña ma[?] de Solira" with the date "quīze" de "otubre" inserted in the proper blank spaces.

Ref: Palau 119107.

18. 1509 [MARINEO, LUCIO, SÍCULO]

Pandit Aragonię veterum primordia regum hoc opus: et forti pręlia gesta manu. [Colophon: Sara-gossa, Jorge Coci, 30 April 1509].

Collation: f°. a⁸, b-h⁶; xlix, [1] leaves (last leaf, blank, wanting). 29cm.

The woodcut illus. on t.-p. (angel bearing shield of Aragon) is from the block used in *Coronica de Aragon* printed in Saragossa, 1498, by Pablo Hurus.

Ref: BM; Haebler, Early printers fig. XVIII; Lyell p. 122; Norton 628; NUC; Palau 152144; Salvá 3019; Sánchez 28 and fig.

19. 1509 ARISTOTELES. SPANISH.

La philosofia moral del Aristotel: es asaber Ethicas: polithicas: y economicas: en romancę. [Colophon: Saragossa, Jorge Coci, 21 de mayo 1509].

Collation: f°. a⁴, b-i⁸, k¹⁰, A-M⁶; [150] leaves. 28cm.

From the Latin version of Leonardo Bruni, with his prologues. Translated into Spanish by Carlos, prince of Viana.

Ref: BM; Gallardo 1590; Heredia 336; HS; Norton 629; Palau 16676; Salvá 3837; Sánchez 29; Vindel, Man. 179.

20. 1509 MENA, JUAN DE.

Las. ccc. cõ. xxiiij. coplas agora nueuamēte añadidas: del famosissimo poeta Juan de Mena con su glosa: τ las cinquenta con su glosa: τ otras obras. [Colo-phon: Saragossa, Jorge Coci, 23 de setiembre 1509].

Collation: f°. π², a-l⁸, ll⁶, m-p⁸, q¹⁰; [2], lxxxviii, [6], lxxxix-cxxx leaves. 29.5cm.

Ex-libris of Charles Fairfax Murray, of the Biblioteca de Salvá, and of Ricardo Heredia.

Ref: HS; Norton 631; NUC; Palau 162691; Salvá 188; Sánchez 30 and fig.

21. 1510 MINGO REVULGO.

Coplas de mingo reuulgo glosadas por Fernãdo de pulgar. [Colophon: Sevilla, Jacobo Cromberger, 10 de febrero 1510].

Collation: 4°. a⁸, b¹²; [20] leaves. 20cm.

Sometimes wrongly ascribed to the editor, Hernando del Pulgar, or to Rodrigo de Cota or Juan de Mena.
Full contemporary blind-stamped calf. Ex-libris of James P. R. Lyell.

Ref: Hazañas I, p. 166; Lyell p. 160-61 and fig. 122; Norton 787; Palau 170278, note; Vindel, Man. 2306; not in Escudero.

22. 1510 PETRARCA, FRANCESCO.
DE REMEDIIS UTRIUSQUE
FORTUNAE. SPANISH.

Francisco Petrarca De los remedios contra prospera y aduersa fortuna . . . [Colophon: Valladolid, Diego de Gumiel, 18 de marzo 1510].

Collation: f°. a-n⁸, o⁶, p-v⁸, u-z⁸, A⁸, B-F⁶; [228] leaves. 30cm.

In this copy, line 22 of [12]ʳ reads "Gozo / la Esperrnça / y la Razon"; as described in Norton 1304, it reads "Gozo / la Esperança / y la Razon". Translated by Francisco de Madrid.

Ref: Alcocer 39; BM; Heredia 348 and fig.; HS; Palau 224246; Salvá 3971.

23. 1510 [FORESTI, JACOPO FILIPPO, DA BERGAMO]

. . . Suma de todas las cronicas del mundo. Llamado en latin Suplementũ cronica♃. [Colophon: Valencia, Jorge Costilla, 11 de setiembre 1510]

Collation: f°. a-v⁸, u⁶, x-z⁸, A-I⁸, L-Z⁸, aa-ii⁸, ll⁸, ✠¹⁰; ccccxlvj, [10] leaves. 30cm.

In this copy, a vertical border-strip of four pieces has been added in the left margin and a strip of three

pieces in the right margin of leaf [1]ᵛ; line 7 of colophon ("el rey dõ Fernando de Aragõ : gouerna"), misplaced in some copies, is in its proper place, and a woodcut ornament (bracket) has been added under the colophon. Translated from the Latin by Narcís Vinyoles.

Ex-libris of the Biblioteca de Salvá, of Ricardo Heredia, and of James P. R. Lyell.

Ref: BM (2 copies, one with and one without the vertical borders on leaf [1]ᵛ); Gallardo 4337 and Serrano p. 93 (with line 7 of colophon in its proper place); Heredia 2910 and fig.; Norton 1225C; Palau 325000; Salvá 2775.

24. 1510 SENECA, LUCIUS ANNAEUS.
SPANISH. DÍAZ DE TOLEDO.

Las epistolas de Seneca cõ vna summa si quier introducion de philosophia moral en romanze con tabla. [Colophon: Toledo, 27 de setiembre 1510].

Collation: f°. a-b⁶, c⁸, d-l⁶, m⁸; lxxiii, [3] leaves. 28.5cm.

Ascribed to the press of Pedro Hagembach's successor. — Cf. Norton 1059. Edited by Perez de Guzman and translated by Pero Díaz de Toledo. — Cf. Palau 30813-15.

Ref: BM (ascribed to the press of Juan Varela); Heredia 2797 and fig.; HS; NUC; Palau 308015; Pérez Pastor, Toledo 46; Salvá 4004; Vindel, Man. 2839.

25. 1511 [BOCCACCIO, GIOVANNI]

Cayda de principes. [Colophon: Toledo, 18 de setiembre 1511].

Collation: f°. π⁴, a-q⁸; [4], cxxvii, [1] leaves (last leaf, blank, wanting). 29cm.

Ascribed to the press of Pedro Hagembach's successor. — Cf. Norton 1072. The illustration of the wheel of Fortune on the title-page is copied from the one of Seville, Ungut and Polono (1495). Edited by Juan Alfonso de Zamora. Translated from the *De casibus virorum illustrium* by Pedro Lopez de Ayala (Books 1-8) and Alfonso de Cartagena (Books 9-10). With this is bound Luis de Soto's *El recebimiento q̃ se hizo al rey don Fernando*, [1513] (see no. 35) Ex-libris of the Huth Library and of James P. R. Lyell.

Ref: BM and Heredia 3502 (ascribed to the press of Juan Alfonso de Zamora); Huth, Sale 799; Lyell p. 92-94 and fig. 73; Norton 1072; Palau 31164; Pérez Pastor, Toledo 48.

26. 1511 CATHOLIC CHURCH. LITURGY AND RITUAL. MISSAL.

Missale romanum. [Colophon: Saragossa, Jorge Coci, 15011 [i.e. 1511].

Collation: 4°. ✠¹⁰, a-z⁸, A-F⁸, G¹⁰; [10], ccxlii leaves. 20cm.

The woodcut illus. on t.-p. (St. Jerome tending the lion) is copied from an Albrecht Dürer block of 1492. — Cf. Lyell p. 140; Crucifixion on leaf cvi^v signed A.G.. Missal of the Hieronymites adapted from the Roman use and edited by Pedro de la Vega. Ex-libris of James P. R. Lyell.

Ref: Norton 649, with signature ✠✠⁶ at end not present in the Houghton copy nor in the following: BM, Palau 173054 (2 copies, one on vellum), Sánchez 44 (impf.).

27. 1512 EL CID CAMPEADOR. SPANISH.

Cronica del famoso cauallero Cid Ruy diez campeador. [Colophon: Burgos, Fadrique de Basilea, 31 de marzo 1512].

Collation: f°. A⁶, B⁸, a-m⁸, n⁶, o⁸, p⁶; [14], cxvi leaves (leaf [14], blank, wanting). 28cm.

Edited by Juan de Velorado, abbot of Cardeña. Most top margins of this copy are repaired, with leaf numbers supplied or retraced in ink.

Ref: BM; Brunet I, col. 1882-83; Gallardo 522; Heredia 3119; HS; Norton 261; NUC; Palau 54485; Salvá 2891, note.

28. 1512 PUBLILIUS SYRUS. SPANISH. DÍAZ DE TOLEDO.

Prouerbios de Seneca. [Colophon: Sevilla, Jacobo Cromberger, 20 de abril 1512].

Collation: f°. a⁶, b-h⁸, i⁶; [6], lx, lxii-lxiij leaves. 30cm.

Translated, with a commentary, by Pero Díaz de Toledo from *Sententiae,* also known as *Proverbiae Senecae;* this collection of aphorisms in prose and verse has been wrongly ascribed to Seneca and to Saint Martinus, abp. of Braga; derived in part from the pseudo-Senecan *De moribus,* it is for the most part by Publilius Syrus. The illus. on [6]^v (St. John the Baptist) is from the block used in the Seville, Ungut and Polono, 1492 edition of Cavalca's *Espejo de la Cruz.* — Cf. Haebler, Early printers p. 124 and fig. xxii.

Ref: Escudero 166; Gallardo 2033; Heredia 2722; NUC; Norton 820; Palau 307848; Salvá 2170.

29. 1512 [NANNI, GIOVANNI, ASCRIBED AUTHOR]

Opuscula in hoc uolumine côtenta. Archilochus de têporum antiquitate & homeris octo. Philonis breuiariũ de têporibus sacrae scripturae . . . Antonius Nebrissêsis . . . dispunxit interpunxit atq3 pro uirili ex inemendato exemplari castigauit & imprimi curauit. [Colophon: Burgos, Fadrique de Basilea, 30 April 1512].

Collation: 4°. a-d⁸; [32, the last blank] leaves. 21.5cm.

A collection of spurious fragments purporting to be the work of Greek and Roman writers; commonly believed to have been forged by Giovanni Nanni.

Ref: BM; Gallardo 2651 (impf.?); Norton 262; NUC; Palau 189301.

30. 1512 [FERNÁNDEZ DE FIGUEROA, MARTÍN]

Conq'sta d'las indias d' Persia ⁊ Arabia q̃ fizo la armada d'l rey don Manuel de Portugal . . . [Colophon: Salamanca, Lorenzo de Liomdedei, 1 de setiembre 1512].

Collation: 4°. a-d⁸; [32] leaves. 18.5cm.

Edited by Juan Agüero de Trasmiera, to whom it is sometimes wrongly ascribed. Ex-libris of the Livraria de Palha.

Ref: Brunet I, 556; J. B. McKenna. *A Spaniard in the Portuguese Indies.* Cambridge, Mass., 1967 (an annotated facsimile edition of this copy); Norton 563; Palau 19506 and 88471; Palha 4139.

31. 1512 CATERINA DA SIENA, SAINT.

Obra delas epistolas y oraciones de . . . sancta catherina de sena . . . Las quales fueron traduzidas d'l toscano en nuestra lengua castellana . . . [Colophon: Alcalá de Henares, Arnao Guillén de Brocar, 22 de noviembre 1512].

Collation: f°. a⁸, b-c⁶, d⁴, A-OO⁸, PP⁶, QQ⁸, RR¹⁰; [24], cccxviii, [2] leaves (last leaf blank). 28cm.

Translation ascribed to Antonio de la Peña. — Cf. Palau 297779. Closely trimmed at top with some leaf numbers missing.

Ref: BM; Catalina 12; Heredia 247; Lyell p. 264 and fig. 211; Norton 15; NUC; Salvá 3999; Vindel, Man. 514.

32. 1512 PETRARCA, FRANCESCO.
TRIONFI. SPANISH.

Francisco Petrarca con los seys triunfos de toscano sacados en castellano con el comento que sobrellos se hizo . . . [Colophon: Logroño, Arnao Guillén de Brocar, 20 de diciembre 1512].

Collation: f°. a-cc⁶, dd⁸, ✠⁶; clxiiij, [6] leaves (last leaf, blank, wanting). 30.5cm.

Translated by Antonio de Obregón y Cereceda. This copy contains at end the 5 leaves of Tabla described in Norton 419B.

Ref: BM; Heredia 1608; HS; Palha 1149; Palau 224253; Salvá 874.

33. 1513 PETRARCA, FRANCESCO.
DE REMEDIIS UTRIUSQUE
FORTUNAE. SPANISH.

Frācisco Petrarca. Delos remedios cōtra ꝑspera ɀ aduersa fortuna . . . [Colophon: Sevilla, Jacobo Cromberger, 3 de febrero 1513].

Collation: f°. A⁶, a-v⁸, x¹⁰; [6], clxix, [1] leaves (last leaf, blank, wanting). 29cm.

Translated by Francisco de Madrid. In this copy, line 6 of [2]ᵛ reads ". . . en otra le trasladã . . .", as described in Norton 834, it reads ". . . en otra trasladã . . .".

Ref: BM; Escudero 173; Heredia 349; Palau 224247; Salvá 3972.

34. 1513 GORDON, BERNARD DE.

Lilio de medicina. Lo contenido eneste presente volumen d' Bernaldo Gordonio es lo siguiente. Primeramente los siete libros que se intitulan Lilio de medicina. Lo segundo: Las tablas delos ingenios. Lo tercero: el regimēto delas agudas. Lo quarto: el Tractado delos niños conel Regimiento del ama. Lo quinto y postrimero: Las pronosticas. Nueuamente enmendado. [Colophon: Toledo, Juan de Villaquirán, 29 de abril 1513].

Collation: f°. a-z⁸, A-G⁸, H⁶; CCXLVI leaves. 29.5cm.

Ref: Fielding H. Garrison. *An introduction to the history of Medicine. 4th ed.* Philadelphia, 1967, p. 164-65; Norton 1105; NUC; Palau 106217; Pérez Pastor, Toledo 63; George Sarton. *Introduction to the history of science.* Baltimore, 1947-62, III, pt.1, p. 873-74; Ernest Wickersheimer. *Dictionnaire biographique des médecins en France au moyen-âge.* Paris, 1936, I, p. 75-76.

35. [1513] [SOTO, LUIS DE]

El recebimiento ꝗ se ħizo al . . . rey don Fernando nřo señor enla villa de Valladolid miercoles por la mañana bispera dela epifania o delos reyes deste año de .d. xiij . . . [Valladolid, 1513].

Collation: f°. [-]²; [2] leaves. 29cm.

Caption title; author named on [2]ᵛ. Ascribed to the Valladolid press of Diego de Gumiel. — Cf. Norton 1313. Bound with Boccaccio's *Cayda de principes*, 1511 (see no. 25). Ex-libris of the Huth library and of James P. R. Lyell.

Ref: Huth, Sale 799; Palau 252244 ([1514]); not in Lyell.

36. 1514 LÓPEZ DE PALACIOS RUBIOS, JUAN.

Libellus de beneficijs in curia vacātibus: per Joannē flauū seu ab aula flaua decretorum doctorē regūq3 ꝯsiliarū edit9. [Colophon: Seville, Juan Varela de Salamanca, 13, April 1514].

Collation: f°. a-b⁶; [12] leaves. 28.5cm.

Ref: Bullón p. 244; B. Col. III, p. 94; Escudero 175; Gallardo 2775; Millares Carlo p. 48; Norton 960; Palau 92107; Vindel, Man. 1025.

37. 1514 CALDERINUS, JOANNES.

Solennis ɀ admodum practicabilis tractatus de ecclesiastico interdicto siue diuinorum: editus per profundissimum . . . dominum Joannem Calderini bononiensem. Nouiter impressum. [Colophon: Salamanca, Lorenzo de Liomdedei, 5 November 1514].

Collation: f°. a-c⁸; [24] leaves. 29cm.

Running title: De censura.

Ref: Norton 570; Palau 39679; Vindel, Man. 376.

38. 1515 BONAVENTURA, SAINT, CARDINAL. SPURIOUS AND DOUBTFUL WORKS.

Psalterium a seraphico sancto bonauentura compilatum in honorem virginis marie. [Colophon: Valencia, Joan Joffre, 4 January 1515].

Collation: 8°. A-Q⁸; cxxvii, [1] leaves (last leaf, blank, wanting). 14.5cm.

Full contemporary blind-tooled calf.

Ref: BM; Norton 1189; Palau 290279; not in Serrano.

39. 1515 LULL, RAMÓN.

Diui Raymũdi Lulli doctoris illuminatiss. Ars inuentiva veritatis. Tabula generalis. Commentum in easdem ipsius raymũdi. [Colophon: Valencia, Diego de Gumiel, 12 February 1515].

Collation: f°. a-l⁸, m-n⁶, A-C⁸, d², D-O⁸, P⁶, q⁶; CXXVII, CXXVI-CXXVII, CXXVII, CXXIX-CXXX, CXXXIII-CCXIX, [7] leaves. 31cm.

Edited by Alonzo de Proza. Ex-libris of William Morris, George Dunn, Ricardo Heredia and James P. R. Lyell.

Ref: BM; *Catalogue of the valuable and extensive library formed by George Dunn . . . sold by auction by Messrs. Sotheby, Wilkinson & Hodge.* London, 1912-17, no. 1340; Heredia 324; Lyell p. 26-28 and fig. 17; Norton 1247; NUC; Palau 143849; Rogent & Durán 53; Serrano p. 208.

40. 1515 DANTE ALIGHIERI. INFERNO.

. . . La traduciõ. del dante de lengua toscana en verso castellano: por el reuerẽdo don po fernãdez de villegas . . . y por el comentado allende d'los otros glosadores . . . [Colophon: Burgos, Fadrique de Basilea, 2 de abril 1515].

Collation: f°. (⁸, a-z⁸, ᴢ⁸, ꜱ⁸, A-O⁸, P-Q⁶; [332] leaves. 30cm.

The first edition of Dante's *Inferno* in Spanish, accompanied by a commentary based on one by Cristoforo Landino.

Ref: BM; Heredia 1604; HS; Lyell p. 84 and fig. 65; Norton 275; Palau 68283; Salvá 559; Vindel, Man. 766.

41. 1515 VALENCIA, SPAIN. LAWS, STATUTES, ETC.

Aureum opus regalium priuilegiorum ciuitatis et regni Valentie cum historia cristianissimi regis Jacobi ipsius primi ꜱquistatoris. [Colophon: Valencia, Diego de Gumiel, 30 October 1515].

Collation: f°. ✠⁶, A⁸, B⁶, C⁸, a-z⁸, A-H⁸; [28], ccxlvii, [1] leaves. 32cm.

Edited by Luis Alanya.

Ref: BM; Heredia 3214; HS; Lyell p. 28 and fig. 18; Norton 1248; Palau 19670; Salvá 3679 (15) (mentions a copy printed on vellum); Serrano p. 208-09.

42. [1515?] CATHOLIC CHURCH. LITURGY AND RITUAL. MISSAL.

Missale sᵽm ritũ ac cõsuetudinẽ insigniũ ecclesia⁊ Oscẽ. ⁊ Jaccẽ. [Saragossa, 1515?].

Collation: 4°. ✠⁸, ✠✠⁴, a-r⁸, s⁴, A-E⁸, F¹², G-N⁸, O⁶; [12], ccliii, [1, blank] leaves. 26cm.

Historiated border on a1ʳ with, at top, a scroll containing the motto of the Saragossan printer Jorge Coci. Leaves [9-12] and ccxlix-liii wanting in this copy. Full contemporary blind-tooled calf.

Ref: Norton 610 (1504 edition) and 684 (this edition); Sánchez 13 (this copy, wrongly assumed to be of the 1504 edition); not in Palau.

43. [CA. 1515] PULGAR, HERNANDO DEL.

Los claros varones despaña: hecho por Fernando del Pulgar . . . [Saragossa, Jorge Coci, ca. 1515].

Collation: 4°. a-f⁸, g¹⁰; [58] leaves. 21cm.

The woodcut illus. on t.-p. bears the monogram of the Saragossan printer Jorge Coci. The Fairfax Murray copy with the ex-libris of James P. R. Lyell.

Ref: Lyell p. 123-25 and fig. 96; Norton 682; not in Palau or Sánchez.

44. [CA. 1515] VALLA, LORENZO.

Expositio laurentij vallensis de elegantia lingue latine in lucem nouiter edita. per . . . Alfonsuz herrariẽsem . . . [Colophon: Salamanca, Lorenzo de Liomdedei] [ca. 1515].

Collation: f°. a-b⁸, c⁴; [20] leaves. 27cm.

Ref: B. Col. VII, p. 121; Norton 577; Palau 349459.

45. 1516 [XIMÉNEZ, FRANCISCO, BP. OF ELNA]

La natura angelica nueuamẽte impressa: emẽdada y corregida. [Colophon: Burgos, Fadrique de Basilea, 30 de mayo 1516].

Collation: f°. aa⁴, a-n⁸, o⁶ (o6 = plate); [4], cix leaves, [1] leaf of plates. 30cm.

Author named on aa4ᵛ.

Ref: Gallardo 4410; NUC; Norton 282; Palau 85189; Vindel, Man. 3252.

46. 1516 SANTILLANA, IÑIGO LÓPEZ DE MENDOZA, MARQUÉS DE.

Prouerbios de dõ yñigo lopez de mendoça. [Colophon: Sevilla, Jacobo Cromberger, 5 de agosto 1516].

Collation: f°. a-d⁸; [32] leaves. 27.5cm.

Illustration and compartment border on t.-p. are from the blocks used in the Seville, 1512 edition. Leaf d3 wanting and supplied in ms.

Ref: Gallardo 2757; Hazañas I, p. 167; Norton 889; Palau 141480, note; not in Escudero.

47. 1516 ENCINA, JUAN DEL.

Cancionero de todas las obras de Juan del enzina: con otras cosas nueuamente añadidas. [Colophon: Saragossa, Jorge Coci, 15 de diciembre 1516].

Collation: f°. a-l⁸, m¹⁰; xcviii leaves. 29cm.

Leaves lxxxix and xcviii are wanting in this copy (leaf lxxxix has been supplied in facsimile). Inserted at end are leaves xcvij-ciiij (signatures n1-8) of the Salamanca, Hans Gysser, 1509 edition of the same work. Ex-libris of Charles Stuart, baron de Rothesay and of James P. R. Lyell.

Ref: BM; Gallardo 2073; Heredia 1852 and Salvá 231 (with [6] leaves of Tragedia at end); HS; Norton 691; NUC; Palau 79576; Sánchez 76; Vindel, Man. 870.

48. 1517 ARAGON. LAWS, STATUTES, ETC.

[Begins, a2ʳ:] Incipiũt fori editi per dominum Jacobum regẽ Aragonum . . . [Colophon: Saragossa, Jorge Coci, 6 April 1517].

Collation: f°. ✠⁶, a-c⁸, d-g⁶·⁸, h-k⁸, l⁶, m-n⁸, o⁶, p-r⁸, ɔ⁶, ʃ⁸, s⁶, t⁸, v⁶, u-z⁸·⁶, ꝛ⁸, ᴐ⁶, ꝭ⁸, ꞇ⁶, st⁸, ss⁶, A-D⁸·⁶, E-F⁸, G⁶, H⁸, a-b⁸; [7], II-CCXXXII, LVIII,

[16] leaves (leaf [7] (1st count), blank, wanting). 29cm.

The full-page woodcut illus. on recto of [1]st leaf (angel facing right, holding shield of Aragon) is a reversed copy of the one found in the Saragossa, 1509 edition of Lucio Marineo's *Pandit Aragoniẹ* (see no. 18). Edited by Miguel de Molino. With this is bound *Fori editi per serenissimũ dominũ Carolũ regẽ Aragonũ*, [Saragossa, 1519?] (see no. 55).

Ref: BM; Norton 696 (8 [?] April 1517); Palau 95554; Sánchez 78.

49. 1517 LÓPEZ DE PALACIOS RUBIOS, JUAN.

Libellus de beneficijs in curia vacantibus: per Joannem lup. d' palacios ruuios decretorum doctorem: regumq3 consiliarium editus. [Colophon: Salamanca, 22 April 1517].

Collation: f°. a⁸, b⁶; [14] leaves. 29cm.

Ascribed to the press of Juan de Porras. — Cf. Norton 505. Bound with his *De iusticia et iure obtẽtionis ac retẽtionis regni Nauarre*, [1517?] (see no. 51).

Ref: B. Col. IV, p. 325-26; BM; Gallardo 2776; Palau 141664.

50. 1517 *Comiença la Cronica del serenissimo rey don Juan el segundo* deste nõbre . . . Logroño, Arnao Guillén de Brocar [colophon: 10 de octubre de 1517].

Collation: f°. ✠¹⁰, A-B⁸, a⁸ (a4 + 1), b-hh⁸, ii⁶; [26], v, v-ccliiij leaves. 32.5cm.

Formerly attributed to Fernán Pérez de Guzmán, the *Cronica* is now generally regarded as a compilation from the works of several authors including Alvar García de Santa María. Edited by Lorenzo Galíndez de Carvajal. — Cf. *Dic. enc. hispano-americano*, Barcelona, 1887-1910, v. 15, p. 114, and James Fitzmaurice-Kelly, *A new history of Spanish literature*, London, 1926, p. 100. The woodcut illus. include a Crucifixion signed I.D., from the block used in the *Missale* published by Arnao Guillén de Brocar in Pamplona, ca. 1501. Ex-libris of James P. R. Lyell.

Ref: BM; Gallardo 3440; HS; Lyell p. 286-88 and fig. 225; Norton 427; NUC; Palau 64966; Salvá 3117.

51. [1517?] LÓPEZ DE PALACIOS RUBIOS, JUAN.

De iusticia et iure obtētionis ac retētionis regni Nauarre liber editus per . . . Jo. lup. de palacios ruuios . . . [Burgos, 1517?].

Collation: f°. a-h⁸, A⁴; [68] leaves. 29cm.

Ascribed to the Burgosian press of Fadrique de Basilea, [1517?]. — Cf. Norton 294. As in the first state described by Norton, h6,7 of this copy are unsigned and uncancelled. With this is bound his *Libellus de beneficijs in curia vacantibus*, Salamanca, 1517 (see no. 49). Ex-Libris of Emmanuel Vicenti.

Ref: Alcocer 32 and fig. ([Valladolid, 1504], [70] leaves, printed on vellum); BM; Bullón p. 272-73 and fig. ([Salamanca, 1514?]); Gallardo 2777 ([Salamanca, 1517]); Millares Carlo, IV, 25 and Palau 141652 [1514?]; NUC; Salvá 3721.

52. 1518 [PADILLA, JUAN DE]

Retablo dela vida de cristo fecho en metro por vn deuoto frayle dela cartuxa . . . [Colophon: Sevilla, Jacobo Cromberger, 26 de noviembre 1518].

Collation: f°. a-h⁸, i-k⁶; vj, [70] leaves. 29cm.

The woodcut illus. on t.-p. is from the block used in the Seville, Ungut and Polono, 1492 edition of Cavalca's *Espejo de la Cruz.* — Cf. Haebler, Early printers p. 124 and pl. xxii. Ex-libris of Alvaro Virgilio Franco Teixeira and of James P. R. Lyell.

Ref: Lyell p. 162-65 and fig. 123-24; Escudero 174, repeated by Palau 208346, cites a Seville edition with title "Retablo . . . en metro castellano de arte mayor por un fraile de la Cartuja", dated 26 de noviembre de 1513; unrecorded elsewhere, it is most probably the above; Norton 910; Vindel, Man. 2064 a-c.

53. 1519 [JOANNES XXI, POPE]

Thesoro delos. pobres en medicína ẓ cirurgia. en romance. Con el tractado del regimiento de sanidad: hecho por Arnaldo de Villanoba. Nuebamente empremido. [Colophon: Granada, Andres de Burgos, 15 de enero 1519].

Collation: f°. a-e⁶; xxx leaves. 39cm.

Author named under pseudonym ("maestre Juliano") on recto of 2d leaf (misnumbered i). A translation of his *Thesaurus pauperum* and of Arnaldus de Villanova's *Regimen sanitatis ad regem Aragonum.* In this copy, the last line of the colophon on xxxʳ reads

"milll [!]"; in Norton 361, it reads "milli". Ex-libris of James P. R. Lyell.

Ref: Lyell p. 252-53 and fig. 199-201; Palau 126027, note.

54. 1519 *Arte de cõfessiõ breue ẓ* mucho prouechosa assi para el cõfessor como para el penitente. [Colophon: Burgos, Alonso de Melgar, 22 de diciembre 1519].

Collation: 8°. a-b⁸; [16] leaves. 15cm.

Ex-libris of Carlos I, king of Portugal and of James P. R. Lyell.

Ref: Lyell p. 199-200 and fig. 157; Norton 324; Palau 17715 (ii); Vindel, Man. 192.

55. [1519?] ARAGON. LAWS, STATUTES, ETC.

[Begins, A2ʳ:] Fori editi per serinissimū dominū Carolū regē Aragonū in curijs generalibus in ciuitate Cesaraugustana . . . [Saragossa, 1519?].

Collation: f°. A⁸; [8] leaves. 29cm.

Attributed to the press of the Saragossan printer Jorge Coci. — Cf. Norton 709. The full-page illus. on recto of first leaf (angel holding shield of Aragon) is from the block used in *Fori editi per dominum Jacobum regē Aragonum,* Saragossa, 1517, with which this copy is bound (see no. 48).

Ref: Norton 709; not in Palau; not in Sánchez.

56. 1520 [HILARIUS (HYMNOLOGIST)]

Aurea expositõ hyño⁊ vna cũ textu: ab Antonij nebrisseñ. castigatione fideliter trāscripta. [Colophon: Saragossa, Jorge Coci, 1 January 1520].

Collation: 4°. a-g⁸, h⁶; [62] leaves. 20cm.

Ref: BM; Norton 710; NUC; Sánchez 92; A. Odriozola. "La caracola del bibliófilo Nebrisense," *Revista de Bibliografía Nacional,* VII (1946), Madrid, 1947, no. 235.

57. 1520 *La institucion dela muy estrecha* y no menos obseruãte orden de cartuxa. y dela vida del excelẽte doctor sant Bruno . . . buelta de latin en romance . . . [Colophon: Sevilla, Juan Varela de Salamanca, 20 de enero 1520].

Collation: 4°. a-b⁸, c⁴; [20] leaves. 20.5cm.

Includes Juan de Padilla's *Coplas* ([16^{v}-19^{v}]).

Ref: BM; Gallardo 4383 and Palau 119944 (10 leaves [!]); Norton 987; not in Escudero.

58. 1520 HIERONYMUS, SAINT.

. . . Epistolas de S. Hieronymo. [Colophon: Valencia, Joan Joffre, 15 de marzo 1520].

Collation: f°. ✠-✠✠^{6}, a-z^{8}, ⁊^{8}, ꝯ^{8}, A-P^{8}, Q-R^{6}; [13], cccxxx, [1] leaves (last leaf, blank, wanting). 30cm.

Translated by Juan de Molina. Ex-libris of Sir William Sterling-Maxwell and of Imrie de Vegh.

Ref: B. Col. III, p. 305-06 (impf.); Norton 1213; Palau 292181; Serrano p. 235; Vindel, Man. 1339.

59. 1520 LIVIUS. SPANISH. VEGA.

. . . Las quatorze decadas de Tito Liuio . . . trasladadas agora nueuamente de latin en nuestra lẽgua castellana. La primera: tercera y quarta enteras segun en latin se hallã: y las otras onze segũ la abreuiaciõ de Lucio floro. [Colophon: Saragossa, Jorge Coci, 24 de mayo 1520.

Collation: f°. ✠✠^{4}, a-v^{8}, x-z^{6}, ⁊^{8}, ꝯ^{6}, ꝶ^{8}, A-V^{8}, *^{6}, aa-xx^{8}, ✠^{8}; [4], cccccxxxiii, [9] leaves. 29.5cm.

Translated by Pedro de la Vega.

Ref: BM; HS; Lyell p. 128-29 and figs. 98, 99 and 101; Norton 712; NUC; Palau 139128; Sánchez 94 (impf.).

60. 1520 [VARTHEMA, LODOVICO DE]

Itinerario del venerable varon micer Luis patricio romano . . . Buelto de latin en romance por Christoual de arcos clerigo. Nunca hasta aqui impresso en lengua castellana. [Colophon: Sevilla, Jacobo Cromberger, 1520].

Collation: f°. a-g^{8}; lv, [1] leaves. 27.5cm.

Author named on ij^{v}. Ex-libris of A. C. Burnell.

Ref: Escudero 204; HS; Heredia 2866 and fig.; Norton 933; Salvá 3757; Vindel, Man. 153.

61. 1521 LULL, RAMÓN.

. . . Blãquerna: qui tracta de sinch estaments de persones: de matrimoni: de religio: de prelatura . . . Hordenat ꝑ lo illuminat doctor: y martyr mestre Ramon Lull. Traduit: y corregit ara nouament dels primers originals: y estampat en llengua valenciana. Ablo Libre de oracions . . . fet per lo matex doctor. [Colophon: Valencia, Joan Joffre, 30 de maig 1521].

Collation: f°. ✠^{8}, A-Q^{8}, R-S^{6}, T^{12}; [9], cli leaves. 28.5cm.

The "Libre d'oracions" (leaves [cxxxxi]-cli) has special t.-p. and colophon dated 12 July 1521.

Ref: BM; Gallardo 2839; Lyell p. 107-11; NUC; Palau 143788; Serrano p. 235-36 (gives date of colophon as 29 [?] May 1521).

62. 1521 [VEGA, PEDRO DE LA]

Flos sanctoruꝫ. La vida de nr̃o señor iesu cristo: ⁊ de su sct'issima madre: ⁊ d'los otros scõs: segũ la ordẽ de sus fiesta^{s} . . . [Colophon: Saragossa, 25 de setiembre 1521].

Collation: f°. ✠^{4}, a-p^{8}; [4], cxx leaves. 33cm.

Author named in colophon. Printed by Jorge Coci. — Cf. Lyell p. 130. Title-page illustration printed in red, blue, yellow and green (faded to brown). The Crucifixion on verso of t.-p. and some of the illus. are from the blocks used in Pablo Hurus' editions of Bernhard von Breydenbach's *Viaje de la tierra sancta*, Saragossa, 1498 and Andrés de Li's *Thesoro de la passion*, Saragossa, 1494. Contains the first part only, the "Hystorias de todas las solẽnidades de nuestro señor . . . jesu christo . . .". Full contemporary brown calf. Ex-libris of Carlos I, king of Portugal and of James P. R. Lyell. Several leaves wormed and repaired.

Ref: Antonio, Nov. II, p. 246; Lyell p. 129-40 and figs. 102-04; Palau 354942; Sánchez 106; Vindel, Man. 3094.

63. 1522 APPIANUS. SPANISH. MOLINA.

. . . Los trivmphos de Apiano. [Colophon: Valencia, Joan Joffre, 20 de agosto 1522].

Collation: f°. ✠-✠✠^{6}, A-R^{8}, S^{10}; [12], cxxxvi, cxxxvi-cxliiii, [1, blank] leaves. 30cm.

Translated by Juan de Molina.

Ref: BM; Heredia 2991; NUC; Palau 13810; Salvá 2777; Serrano p. 236.

64. 1514-17 [i.e. 1522?] BIBLE. POLYGLOT. COMPLUTENSIAN.

[Libri Veteris ac Novi Testamenti multiplici lingua impressi] [Alcalá de Henares, Arnao Guillén de Brocar, 1514-17 [i.e. 1522?].

f°. 6v. 37cm.

Though the colophons are variously dated 1514 to 1517, the 6 volumes of the Complutensian polyglot Bible were apparently not published until late 1521 or 1522. — Cf. T. H. Darlow and H. F. Moule. *Historical catalogue of the printed editions of Holy Scripture in the library of the British and foreign Bible Society.* London, 1903, no. 1412, p. 3, and Norton 27, p. 14 (General Note).

V. 1-4: . . . Vetus testamentū multiplici lingua nūc primo impressum. Et imprimis Pentateuchus hebraico greco atq3 chaldaico idiomate. Adiūcta vnicuiq3 sua latina interpretatione. [Colophon at end of v. 4: 10 July 1517].

Collations:
V.1: ✠⁸, a-zz⁶, ȝ ȝ⁶, ꝛ ꝛ⁸, a² [errata]; [300] leaves (leaf [1], presumably a cancelled blank, wanting).
V.2: π², a-tt⁶, vv⁴, a² [errata]; [260] leaves.
V.3: aaa-ddd⁶, eee⁴, Aaa-Bbb⁶, Ccc⁴, Ddd-Hhh⁶, Iii⁴, a-i⁶, k⁴, l-o⁶, p⁸, A-E⁶, F⁴, a² [errata]; [204] leaves (leaves [136] and 204] blank).
V.4: a-z⁶, aa-oo⁶, pp⁴, A-F⁶, G⁴, a² [errata]; [268] leaves.

In most copies of v.1, leaf [7]ᵛ contains the papal privilege dated 22 March 1520; in this copy, however, [7]ᵛ is blank as described in Norton 27C; the errata leaves of v.1-4 are wanting in this copy.

V.5: . . . Nouum testamentum grece ꝛ latine in academia complutensi nouiter impressum . . . [Colophon: 10 January 1514].

Collation: a⁴, A-Q⁶, α⁶, R-LL⁶, MM⁸, a¹⁰, a-f⁶, g⁴; [272] leaves (last leaf blank).

V.6: . . . Vocabularium hebraicum atq3 chaldaicū totius veteris testamenti cū alijs tractatibus prout infra in prefatione continetur in academia complutensi nouiter impressum. [Colophons: 17 March and 31 May 1515].

Collation: π², A-EE⁶, FF⁴, a⁸, A-D⁶, E², A-B⁶, C⁴; [2, the second blank], clxxij, [34], xv, [1, blank] leaves.

Ref: BM; Catalina 19; B. Hall. *The great polyglot Bibles.* San Francisco, 1966; HS; Lyell, Ximenes p. 24-51 and Appendix A; Norton 27A-G; NUC; Palau 28930.

65. 1524 PETRARCA, FRANCESCO. DE REMEDIIS UTRIUSQUE FORTUNAE. SPANISH.

Frãcisco petrarcha de los rremedios [!] contra prospa ꝛ aduersa fortuna. En romance. [Colophon: Sevilla, Juan Varela de Salamanca, 12 de enero 1524].

Collation: f°. A⁴, a-v⁸, x¹⁰ (x10=plate); [4], clxix leaves, [1] leaf of plates. 28.5cm.

Translated by Francisco de Madrid.

Ref: J. Hazañas y la Rua. *La imprenta en Sevilla, ensayo de una historia de la tipografía sevillana.* Sevilla, 1892, p. 124; Lyell p. 182; Palau 224251; not in Escudero.

66. 1524 [MARINEO, LUCIO, SÍCULO]

Cronica Daragon. [Colophon: Valencia, Joan Joffre, 9 de junio 1524].

Collation: f°. A-G⁸, H-I⁶; lxvii, [1] leaves. 29cm.

Translated from his *Pandit Aragonię,* 1509 (see no. 18) by Juan de Molina, whose name appears in the dedication. Ex-libris of Henry Edward Bunbury.

Ref: BM; Heredia 3194; HS; NUC; Palau 152145; Salvá 3020; Serrano p. 236.

67. [1524] ENZINAS, FERDINAND DE.

Ad illvstrissimvm excellentissimumq3 dominum Ferdinandum de Aragonia Calabriae ducē Ferdinandi de Enzinas epistola: qua comprobatur: vana esse quae vulgus astrologorum toti orbi cōminatur: ex eo qui futurus est oĩum planetarū conuentu in signo piscium anno Dñi. 1524. . . . [Colophon: Alcalá de Henares, Arnao Guillén de Brocar] [1524].

Collation: 4°. a⁸; [8] leaves. 19.5cm.

Ref: Catalina 68; G. Hellmann. *Beiträge zur Geschichte der Meteorologie.* Berlin, 1914, p. 33 (with date [1523]); Lyell p. 264-66 and fig. 212; Palau 80136.

68. 1525 AUGUSTINUS, AURELIUS, SAINT, BP. OF HIPPO.

Diui aurelij Augustini . . . Meditationes. Soliloquia. Manuale. atq3 Psalterium. feliciter incipit. [Colophon: Valencia, Joan Joffre, 22 February] 1525.

Collation: 8°. ✠⁸, A-Z⁸, a-b⁸; [8], cxcix, [1, blank] leaves. 17.5 cm.

Ex-libris of James P. R. Lyell.

Ref: Lyell p. 111 and fig. 84; Palau 289316; not in Serrano.

69. 1525 PALMERIN DE OLIVA. SPANISH.

Palmerin de Oliva. Libro del famoso ⁊ muy efforçado cauallero Palmerin de Oliva . . . Nueuamente corregido ⁊ hystoriado. [Colophon: Sevilla, Juan Varela de Salamanca, 30 de mayo 1525].

Collation: f°. a-v⁸; clx leaves. 29.5cm.

Ex-libris of François Florentin Achille, baron Seillière (Bibliothèque de Mello).

Ref: BM; Escudero 242; HS; Hazañas II, p. 83; NUC; Palau 210470.

70. 1525 CATHOLIC CHURCH. LITURGY AND RITUAL. MISSAL.

Missale secundū consuetudinē burgeñ ecclesię nūc denuo impressu3 atq3 correctū. [Colophon: Burgos, Miguel de Eguia, May 1525].

Collation: f°. ✠⁸, a-i⁸, k¹⁰, l⁸, m¹⁴, n-s⁸, t-v¹⁰, x-y⁸, z⁴ (z4 = plate), ✠✠¹⁰, A-G⁸, H⁴, J-L⁸, M-N⁶; [8], clxxxj (i.e. 191), [10], clxxxij-cclxxvj (i.e. 192-287) leaves, [1] leaf of plates. 33cm.

Numerous errors in foliation. Illustration on t.-p. (Annunciation) and tail-piece on recto of last leaf (Immaculate Conception) signed D.N.; the plate (Last Judgment) and a full page illus. on y3ʳ (Crucifixion) are signed I.D.. They are from the blocks used in the *Constitutiones prouinciales* and the *Missale* published by Arnao Guillén de Brocar in Pamplona, 1501; Brocar also used the Crucifixion block in the *Cronica del serenissimo rey don Juan el segundo*, Logroño, 1517 (see no. 50).

Ref: Not in BM, Gallardo, NUC or Palau; Lyell discusses the 1517 edition of the Cronica on p. 286 and reproduces the Crucifixion (fig. 225).

71. 1525 NOLA, ROBERTO DE.

Libro de cozina cōpuesto por maestre Ruberto de Nola . . . Muy bien corregido y emendado . . . [Colophon: Toledo, Ramon de Petras, 21 de noviembre 1525].

Collation: 4°. a-h⁸, i¹⁰ (i10 = plate); lxxj, [2] leaves, [1] leaf of plates. 20cm.

Ex-libris of James P. R. Lyell.

Ref: Aguílo 2008; Brunet IV, col. 94; Gallardo 3223; Lyell p. 222 and fig. 176 and 177; NUC; Palau 192534; Pérez Pastor, Toledo 109; Vicaire col. 625, note.

72. 1526 VERINO, MICHELE.

Michaelis Verini poetae christianissimi de puerorum moribus disticha: cum luculento ac nouo Martini Juarrae cantabrici commentario. [Colophon: Barcelona, Johann Rosembach, 1 January 1526].

Collation: 4°. a-f⁸, g⁶, h⁴; [58] leaves. 21.5cm.

Ex-libris of James P. R. Lyell.

Ref: Brunet, Supp. II, col 868; Heredia 1568; Lyell p. 50; NUC; Palau 360417.

73. 1526 HIERONYMUS, SAINT.

[Epistolas de sant Hieronimo . . .] [Colophon: Valencia, Jorge Costilla, 30 de enero 1526].

Collation: f°. ✠¹⁰, a-z⁸, ⁊⁸, ꝛ⁸, A-L⁸, M-N⁶; [10], cccii (i.e. 300) leaves. 28.5cm.

Numerous errors in foliation include leaf ccc misnumbered cccii. Translated by Juan de Molina. Ex-libris of the Noviciaria de Santa Cruz de Coimbra. Title-page wanting in this copy; title transcribed from the British Museum Catalogue; tear in leaf lxxx, slightly affecting text.

Ref: BM; Palau 292182; not in Serrano.

74. 1526 [TORRE, ALFONSO DE LA]

Visiō delectable dela philosophia ⁊ artes liberales: metaphisica: y philosophia moral. [Colophon: Sevilla, Jacobo & Juan Cromberger, 16 de junio 1526].

Collation: f°. a-k⁸; lxxx leaves. 28.5cm.

Ex-libris of Sir William Sterling-Maxwell.

Ref: BM; Brunet V, col. 886; Escudero 251; HS; Heredia 3563 and fig.; Lyell p. 166; NUC (microfilm); Palau 335324; Salvá 2434 and fig.

75. 1526 EL CID CAMPEADOR. SPANISH.

Coronica del muy esforçado ⁊ inuencible cauallero el Cid ruy diaz campeador delas Españas. [Colophon: Toledo, Miguel de Eguia, 2 de julio 1526].

Collation: 4°. a-e⁸, f¹² (f12 = plate); 51 leaves, [1] leaf of plates. 21cm.

Ex-libris of the Livraria de Palha.

Ref: Brunet I, col. 1881-82; Gallardo 524 (with title: . . . el Cid ruy diaz emperador [!] . . .); HS; Palau 54487; Palha 3911; Pérez Pastor, Toledo 118; Salvá 1579.

76. 1526 CATHOLIC CHURCH. LITURGY AND RITUAL. RITUAL.

Manuale s'm consuetudinem astoricĕn. ecclesie quam optime ordinatum nouiter impressum. [Colophon: León, at the expense of Juan de León, 5 October] 1526.

Collation: 4°. ✠⁶, a-p⁸; [6], xcv, xcv-cxix leaves. 27cm.

Ref: not in BM, NUC, Palau, or in Ramón Alvarez de la Braña's *Catálogos de la Biblioteca provincial de Léon*, 2a ed. León, 1897.

77. 1527 *Historia de sant Juan baptista:* alegado de latere de jesu xp̄o saluador del mūdo ⁊ su embaxador . . . [Colophon: Valencia, Joan Joffre, 14 de enero 1527].

Collation: 4°. A¹⁶; [16] leaves. 18.5cm.

Ex-libris of the Biblioteca de Salvá and of Ricardo Heredia.

Ref: Heredia 69 and fig.; Palau 115304; Salvá 3454; Serrano p. 237.

78. 1528 CIRUELO, PEDRO.

Expositio libri missalis peregregia: nuper edita ex officina sapientissimi . . . Petri Cirueli . . . Addita sunt ⁊ tria eiusdem autoris opuscula. De arte predicandi. De arte memorãdi. Et de correctione kalendarij . . . [Colophon: Alcalá de Henares, Miguel de Eguia, 6 February 1528].

Collation: f°. a-b⁶, c-z⁸, &⁸, ꝛ⁸, A-J⁸, K⁶, L⁸; cclxxxj (i.e. 280), [2] leaves. 30.5cm.

Numerous errors in foliation. Ex-libris of James P. R. Lyell.

Ref: BM; Catalina 104; Gallardo 1830; Lyell p.268-69 and fig. 213; Palau 54933.

79. 1528 CATHOLIC CHURCH. LITURGY AND RITUAL. SACRAMENTARY.

Sacramentale. [Colophon: Saragossa, Jorge Coci, 23 de marzo 1528].

Collation: 4°. a-l⁸, m⁴; [92] leaves (last leaf blank). 22.5cm.

This copy is printed on vellum. Ex-libris of Charles Louis de Bourbon, comte de Villafranca, and of James P. R. Lyell.

Ref: BM, Palau 284072, and Sánchez 141 (all on paper).

80. 1528 [DAVID DE AUGUSTA]

Libro llamado forma de los nouicios cōpuesto por el serafico doctor sant buenauentura . . . [Colophon: Sevilla, Jacobo Cromberger, en fin del mes de abril] 1528.

Collation: f°. ✠⁶, a-s⁸, t¹⁰; [6], cliij, [1] leaves (leaf [6] and last leaf, blank, wanting). 30cm.

"Forma de los novicios" (j-ciiijᵛ), wrongly attributed to St. Bonaventura, is a translation of David de Augusta's *De exterioris et interioris compositione* and *De septem processibus religiosorum.* "Imagen de vida" (ciiijᵛ-cxxxvʳ) and "Arbol de la vida" (cxljʳ-cliiijᵛ) are translations of St. Bonaventura's *Soliloquium de quatuor mentalibus exercitiis* and of *Lignum vitae.* "De vna breue informaciō para aꝗl ꝗ por buena vida dessea saber la verdadera sabiduria" (cxxxvʳ-cxljʳ) is a translation of Isaac of Nineveh's *Liber de contemptu mundi,* sometimes wrongly ascribed to Isaac of Antioch. Full contemporary calf with blind-stamped compartment border on covers. Title-page repaired and mounted on stub. Ex-libris of the Livraria de Alcobaça.

Ref: Escudero 281; Hazañas II, p. 251; Palau 290237.

81. 1528 MENA, JUAN DE.

Copilacion de todas las obras del famosissimo poeta Juan de mena: cōuiene saber. Las. ccc. con otras. xxiiij. coplas y su glosa: y la corōaciō y las coplas de los siete peccados mortales cō otras cartas y coplas y canciones suyas. Agora nueuamēte añadidas. [Colophon: Sevilla, Juan Varela de Salamanca, 20 de mayo, 16 de mayo] 1528.

Collation: f°. 2pts in IV. 29cm.
Pt.1: a-n⁸; ciiij leaves.
Pt.2: a-b⁸, c¹⁰; xxvj leaves.

Part 2 has special t.-p.: La coronacion . . . con otras coplas añadidas a la fin . . . . Ex-libris of the Biblioteca Heberiana, of the Biblioteca de Salvá and of Ricardo Heredia.

Ref: Escudero 272; Heredia 1822 and figures; HS; NUC; Palau 162695; Salvá 790.

82. 1528 BOCCACCIO, GIOVANNI.

Libro de Juã bocacio que tracta delas illustres mugeres. [Colophon: Sevilla, Jacobo Cromberger, 23 de junio 1528].

Collation: f°. a-k⁸, l¹⁰; lxxxvj, [4] leaves (last leaf, blank, wanting). 29cm.

Ex-libris of the Biblioteca de Salvá.

Ref: BM; Escudero 270; HS; Heredia 3503; Lyell p. 165; NUC; Palau 31162; Salvá 1716.

83. [1528?] FRIAS, MARTINO DE.

Tractatus perutilis Martini de Frias theologie in Salmanticensi academia professoris. . . . [Burgos, Juan de Junta, 1528?].

Collation: 4°. ✠², a¹⁰, b-n⁸, A-D⁸, E⁴; [12], xcvi, xxxiiij, [2] leaves. 20cm.

Printer named on a1ᵛ. "Tratado del modo y estilo que en la visitacion ordinaria se a de tener", xxxiiij leaves (3d count).

Ref: Palau 95011; not in BM, Gallardo or NUC.

84. 1529 [BARTHOLOMAEUS ANGLICUS]

Libro de proprietatibus rerum en romance. Hystoria natural: do se tratã las ppiedades d'todas las cosas . . . [Colophon: Toledo, Gaspar de Avila, 10 de julio 1529].

Collation: f°. A⁶, A-Y⁸, a-v⁸, x⁴; [346] leaves. 30.5cm.

Translated by Vicente de Burgos. Ex-libris of François Florentin Achille, baron Seillière (Bibliothèque de Mello).

Ref: BM; Heredia 8269 (impf.); HS (impf.); NUC; Palau 102874; Pérez Pastor, Toledo 151.

85. 1529 CAESAR. SPANISH. LÓPEZ DE TOLEDO.

Commentarios de Cayo Julio Cesar . . . nueuamẽte impressos y corregidos. [Colophon: Alcalá de Hen-

ares, Miguel de Eguia, 1 de agosto] 1529.

Collation: f°. π¹, ✠⁸ (-✠8 = π1), A-U⁸, X-Y⁴; [9], ij-clxviij leaves (✠1-4 missigned ✠2-5; leaf [9], blank, wanting). 29cm.

Translated by Diego López de Toledo. Contemporary vellum wrappers, cloth ties. Ex-libris of Pedro de Sedano and of James P. R. Lyell. Inserted at front of this copy is an A.L.s. (Théophile Homolle of the Bibliothèque Nationale) to James P. R. Lyell, Paris, 23 Oct. 1917, describing the Bibliothèque Nationale copy.

Ref: Catalina 113; Heredia 2998 (le f. A1, qui manque jusqu'à ce jour . . . a été remplacé par un feuillet blanc, tous les exemplaires connus ayant ce premier f. blanc); Lyell p. 270 and fig. 215; NUC; Palau 54138; Salvá 2779 (impf.).

86. 1529 [GUEVARA, ANTONIO DE]

Libro aureo de Marco aurelio . . . Nueuamente impresso. [Saragossa, Jorge Coci] 1529.

Collation: f°. a-i⁸, k-l⁶; 81, [3] leaves (last leaf, blank, wanting). 30.5cm.

Title within woodcut compartment border including at top the monogram of the Saragossan printer Jorge Coci.

Ref: Gómez Canedo 3; HS; Palau 110084; Sánchez 163; Philip A. Turner. "The libro áureo and the Relox of A. de Guevara," *Harvard Library Bulletin,* vol. V, no. 1, Winter 1951, p. 63-76.

87. 1530 CATHOLIC CHURCH. LITURGY AND RITUAL. RITUAL.

Ordinariũ sacramẽtorũ secũdum ritũ z cõsuetudinẽ sct'e metropolis eccl'ie Tarracoñ . . . [Colophon: Barcelona, Johann Rosembach, 7 February 1530].

Collation: 4°. π², a-f⁸, g-i⁴, k⁸, l⁴, m-q⁸, r⁴, ſ⁸, s-v⁸, x¹⁰; [2], clvii, [1] leaves. 21cm.

The full-page woodcut Crucifixion on verso of t.-p. is from the block used in Rosembach's 1509 edition of the *Missale parvum.* Leaf xcv, misnumbered xci in this copy, is correctly numbered in another Houghton copy.

Ref: Aguiló 73; BM; Palau 203521.

88. 1532 HIERONYMUS, SAINT.

. . .Epistolas del glorioso dotor sant Hieronymo.

Agora nueuamente impresso y emendado. [Colophon: Sevilla, Juan Varela de Salamanca, 25 de junio] 1532.

Collation: f°. ✠⁸, a-z⁸, ₹⁸, A-G⁸; cclv, [1] leaves. 30.5cm.

Woodcut illus. on t.-p. signed Php(?); full-page dotted print of St. Jerome and the lion on verso of t.-p. assigned to the neighborhood of Cologne, ca. 1470, and probably introduced in Spain by a German printer. — Cf. Arthur M. Hind. *An introduction to a history of woodcut.* London, 1935, I, p. 194; W. L. Schreiber. *Manuel de l'amateur de la gravure sur bois et sur métal au XVe siècle.* Berlin, 1893, III, 2672, p. 168 notes the same print (troisième état) in a Valencia, 1520 edition of the *Epistolas.* Translated by Juan de Molina.

Ref: Escudero 309; Hazañas II, p. 85; Lyell p. 168, 172 and fig. 131 (discusses the dotted print of St. Jerome in the Seville, 1537 edition); Palau 292183.

89. 1532 Petrarca, Francesco. Trionfi. Spanish.

Triumphos de Petrarca. Translacion d'los seys triumfos de Frãcisco petrarca de toscano en castellão: fecho por antonio de obregõ . . . Agora de nueuo emẽdada. [Colophon: Sevilla, Juan Varela de Salamanca, 5 de setiembre 1532].

Collation: f°. a-s⁸, t-v⁶; clvj leaves. 27.5cm.

The illustrative material is printed from the blocks used in Varela's Seville, 1526 edition. — Cf. Heredia 1610. Ex-libris of Carlos I, king of Portugal and of James P. R. Lyell.

Ref: BM; Escudero 317; Gallardo 3253; HS; Lyell p. 182 and fig. 141; NUC; Palau 224256; Salvá 876.

90. 1534 Malta, Knights of.

. . .Stabilimenta militum sacri ordinis diui Joannis hierosolymitani: vna cum bulla ipsis concessa. A summo pontifice Claemente .vij. [Colophon: Salamanca, Juan de Junta, 3 July 1534].

Collation: f°. A-K⁸; lxvij, [13] leaves. 29.5cm.

Edited by Alvaro Perez de Grado. Autograph signature of Alvaro Perez de Grado on K1ᵛ. Full contemporary brown calf gilt-tooled with arabesques and floral ornaments.

Ref: Ferdinand de Hellwald. *Bibliographie méthodique de l'ordre souv. de St. Jean de Jerusalem.* Rome, 1885, p. 214; Palau 321844.

91. 1535 Bible. N.T. Epistles and Gospels, Liturgical. Spanish.

Epistolas i euãgelios por todo el año cõ sus dotrinas y sermones segun la reformacion ₹ interpretacion que desta obra hiẑo fray Ambrosio montesino . . . [Colophon: Toledo, Juan de Villaquirán & Juan de Ayala, 27 de octubre] 1535.

Collation: f°. ✠⁶, A-GG⁸; [6], ccxxxix, [1] leaves. 28cm.

Title within ornamental border signed IDV (i.e. Juan de Vingles). — Cf. Nagler III, 2247; full-page Crucifixion signed D.N. on ✠6ᵛ.

Ref: Lyell p. 220-21 and fig. 172-74; NUC (this copy); Palau 178948; Pérez Pastor, Toledo 164.

92 1535 Spain. Cortes.

. . . Quaderno de las cortes: que en Valladolid tuuo su magestad del emperador y rey nuestro señor el año de. 1523. años. Enel qual ay muchas leyes ₹ decissiones nueuas . . . [Colophon: Burgos, Juan de Junta, 20 de noviembre 1535].

Collation: f°. a-c⁶; [18] leaves. 27.5cm.

In this copy, the woodcut illus. on t.-p. is surrounded by a three-sided woodcut compartment border; another Harvard copy (Law School) with variant title ". . . el año de. M.d. xxiij. años. Enel q̃l . . ." below the same woodcut illus. is surrounded by a four-sided compartment border; signatures a and b have been reset.

Ref: BM; NUC; Palau 63142.

93. [ca. 1535] Diaz Tanco de Frejenal, Vasco.

Los veinte triumphos hechos por Vasco Diaz de Frexenal. [Valencia? ca. 1535].

Collation: 4°. a-r⁸, s-t⁴; cxl, [4] leaves. 21.5cm.

Possibly printed at Valencia by the author himself. — Cf. his *Palinodia de los Turcos. Reimpresión facsimilar de la rarísima edicion de Orense,* 1547. *Introduccion bibliográfica por A. Rodrígues-Moñino,* [Badajoz], 1947, no. 4, p. 34. Ex-libris of Sir William Sterling-Maxwell. Title-page mutilated and part of woodcut border restored in pen and ink.

Ref: BM (impf.); Gallardo 2044; HS; Heredia 1854, 3689; NUC; Palau 72899.

94. 1536 CATHOLIC CHURCH. LITURGY AND RITUAL. RITUAL.

. . . Ordo ad cõficiēdū sanctū chrisma ⁊ oleū pro sacerdotib9 episcopo minitrãtib9. [Colophon: Palencia, Diego de Cordova, January 1536].

Collation: 4°. a-b⁸, c⁶; xxij leaves. 25cm.

Episcopal arms of Francisco de Mendoza at head of title with legend in letterpress "Hec sunt Mendocie. Capreeq3 insignia gentis . . . ." Inscribed on front fly leaf: Philip Hofer, esq. with very kind regards from James P. R. Lyell. Oxford, July 1933.

Ref: Palau 203549; not in BM, NUC or Salvá.

95. 1536 JOSEPHUS, FLAVIUS. SPANISH. PALENCIA.

Josepho de belo judayco. Los siete libros . . . [Colophon: Sevilla, Juan Cromberger, 22 de junio] 1536.

Collation: f°. a-r⁸; cxxxvj leaves. 27.5cm.

Title within woodcut compartment border including printer's mark at foot and initials S.M.D. within cartouche. Translated by Alfonso de Palencia from Rufinus' Latin version emended by Erasmus. Ex-libris of Carlos I, king of Portugal and of James P. R. Lyell.

Ref: BM; Escudero 378; Heredia 2979; Lyell p. 168 and fig. 129; Palau 125052, note; Salvá 2784.

96. 1537 INQUISITION. SPAIN.

Copilacion delas instructiones del Officio dela sancta Inquisicion hechas por el muy reuerendo señor fray Thomas de Torquemada . . . [Colophon: Granada, 29 de setiembre 1537].

Collation: f°. A-C⁶, D⁸; [26] leaves. 32cm.

T.-p. within woodcut compartment border including the letter Y used by Sancho de Lebrija to identify his work; printer's mark of the same at head of colophon. — Cf. Vindel, Escudos p. 105.

Ref: Heredia 2932; HS; NUC; Palau 335036; Salvá 3691.

97. 1537 [ARANDA, ANTONIO DE]

Verdadera informaciõ d'la tierra santa segũ la disposiciõ en q̃ eneste año de M.D.xxx. el auctor la vio y passeo . . . [Colophon: Toledo, Juan de Ayala, 15 de diciembre 1537].

Collation: 4°. a-o⁸, p⁴; cxv, [1] leaves (last leaf blank). 21cm.

The full-page Crucifixion signed D.N. on verso of t.-p. is from the block used in the Toledo, 1535 edition of *Epistolas i euãgelios por todo el año* (see no. 91). Full contemporary blind- and gold-tooled black morocco, gauffered edges. Ex-libris of James P. R. Lyell.

Ref: BM; Lyell p.221 and fig. 172 (describes Crucifixion); Palau 14902, note; Pérez Pastor, Toledo 169 (impf.).

98. 1537 BIBLE. N.T. EPISTLES AND GOSPELS, LITURGICAL. SPANISH.

Epistolas y euangelios por todo el año cõ sus doctrinas y sermones d' la correcion de fray Ambrosio mõtesino: los mas copiosos q̃ fasta agora se hã impresso . . . [Colophon: Sevilla, Juan Cromberger] 1537.

Collation: f°. ✠⁶, a-z⁸, &⁸, ꝛ⁸, ꝝ⁸, A-C⁸, D⁶; [6], ccxxxvij, [1] leaves. 30.5cm.

Title-page mounted on stub with fore-edge torn and repaired; upper part of last leaf mutilated.

Ref: Palau 178949; not in Escudero.

99. 1537 [GUEVARA, ANTONIO DE, BP.]

Marco aurelio cõel Relox de principes . . . [Colophon: Sevilla, Juan Cromberger, 1537].

Collation: f°. ✠¹⁰, a-z⁸, ꝛ⁸, ꝛ⁸, ꝝ⁸, A⁶, B-D⁸; [10], ccxxxviij leaves. 31cm.

Leaves cviii and cix (o4.5) wanting. Full contemporary stamped calf.

Ref: BM; Escudero 382; Gómez Canedo 111; NUC; Palau 110097.

100. 1537. HIERONYMUS, SAINT.

Epistolas del glorioso doctor sant Hieronimo. Agora nueuamente impressas. [Colophon: Sevilla, Juan Cromberger] 1537.

Collation: f°. ✠⁸, a-z⁸, ꝛ⁸, ꝛ⁸, ꝝ⁸, A-E⁸; [8], ccxlvij, [1] leaves. 29cm.

The full-page dotted print of St. Jerome and the lion on ✠8ᵛ is from the plate (Cologne? ca. 1470) used in the Seville, Juan Varela de Salamanca, 1532 edition (see no. 88). Translated by Juan de Molina. Tear in leaf xciij, slightly affecting text. Ex-libris of Carlos I, king of Portugal and of James P. R. Lyell.

Ref: Lyell p. 168, 172 and fig. 130-31; NUC; Palau 292184; not in Escudero.

101. 1538 CHIRINO, ALONSO.

Tractado llamado menor daño de medicina: compuesto por el muy famoso maestro Alonso Chirino: fisico del rey don Juan el segundo de Castilla . . . [Colophon: Sevilla, Juan Cromberger, 8 de enero 1538].

Collation: f°. a-f⁸; xxxvi leaves. 30.5cm.

Ref: Escudero 389; Palau 67857.

102. 1538 INFANTE, JUAN.

Forma libelandi compuesta por el famoso doctor el doctor Infante. [Colophon: Sevilla, Juan Cromberger, 12 de marzo 1538].

Collation: f°. a¹⁴; [14] leaves. 27.5cm.

The illustration on t.-p. (judge, two scribes and pleaders beneath twin arches) is from the same block as in the Seville, Stanislao Polono, 1500 edition of this work.

Ref: Palau 119234; Haebler 324 and Vindel, Arte V, 134 (1500 edition); not in Escudero.

103. 1538 [VALERA, DIEGO DE]

La cronica de España abreuiada por mandado dela muy poderosa señora doña Isabel reyna de Castilla. ƈc. [Colophon: Sevilla, Juan Cromberger, 12 de julio 1538].

Collation: f°. ✙⁶, a-l⁸, m-n⁶; [6], c leaves. 30cm.

Author named on ✙6ᵛ. Title-page and several leaves torn and repaired at fore-edge, slightly affecting border and text. Ex-libris of Boies Penrose II.

Ref: Escudero 395; Palau 348598.

104. 1538 PADILLA, LORENZO DE.

Catalogo delos santos de España colegido por dõ Lorenço de Padilla . . . [Colophon: Toledo, Fernando de Sancta Catalina, 12 de diciembre 1538].

Collation: f°. ✙⁴ (✙4 = plate), A⁸, B-G⁶; [3], xliij, [1] leaves (last leaf, blank, wanting), [1] leaf of plates. 28cm.

Bound in are extra copies of leaves xxxiiij and xxxvij (F2.5). The leaf of plates, a woodcut Crucifixion mentioned in Pérez Pastor, Toledo 178, is wanting in this copy.

Ref: NUC; Palau 208366.

105. 1539 MARINEO, LUCIO, SÍCULO.

Obra compuesta por Lucio Marineo Siculo coronista d' sus majestades de las cosas memorables de España. [Colophon: Alcalá de Henares, Juan de Brocar, 14 de julio] 1539.

Collation: f°. ✙⁶, ✙✙⁴, a-z⁸, A⁸; [10], cxcij leaves. 28.5cm.

Translated from his *De rebus Hispaniae memorabilibus.* Ex-libris of James P. R. Lyell.

Ref: BM; Brunet III, col. 1432 ("demi-goth [!]"); Catalina 167; Grässe IV, p. 400; Harrisse 226; Heredia 3098; HS; Lyell p. 272; Palau 152137; Prescott II, p. 194, note 14; Salvá 3024.

106. 1540 *Coronica del santo rey* dõ *fernando tercero* . . . [Colophon: Salamanca, Pedro de Castro, 8 de noviembre] 1540.

Collation: f°. A-E⁸, F⁴; xliij, [1] leaves. 28cm.

Title and vignette on t.-p. within woodcut compartment border with lower element signed IDV (i.e. Juan de Vingles). — Cf. Nagler III, 2247.

Ref: Palau 64934.

107. 1540 DESCOUSU, CELSE HUGUES.

Las leyes de todos los reynos de Ca[stilla]: abreuiadas y reduzidas en forma de repertorio dec[isiuo] . . . por Hugo de Celso . . . [Colophon: Alcalá de Henares, Juan de Brocar, 20 de noviembre] 1540.

Collation: f°. AA⁸, a-z⁸, A-X⁸; [8], ccclij leaves. 30.5cm.

Two words in the title have been partially erased and some of the letters incorrectly supplied in ms. Ex-libris of Carlos I, king of Portugal.

Ref: Catalina 175; HS; NUC; Palau 51240, note.

108. 1541 PETRARCA, FRANCESCO. TRIONFI. SPANISH.

Triumphos de Petrarca. Translacion delos seys triumphos . . . de toscano en castellano: fecho por

Antonio de obregõ . . . Agora de nueuo emendada. [Colophon: Valladolid, Juan de Villaquirán, 31 de mayo] 1541.

Collation: f°. a-s⁸, t¹⁰, v⁸, x⁶; clij (i.e. clxij), [6] leaves. 28.5cm.

Leaf clxij misnumbered clij. In this copy, the first name of the printer in the colophon reads "Juan" and leaf xcii is misnumbered lxxxvij; in another Houghton copy, the first name of the printer in the colophon reads "Jnan" [!] and leaf xcij is correctly numbered. Full contemporary brown calf with the arms and motto ("Hasta quando señor") of Sir William Pickering stamped in gilt and enameled in red on covers.

Ref: NUC (with "Jnan" [!] in colophon); Palau 224257 and Salvá 876, note (with "Juan" in colophon).

109. 1541 HIERONYMUS, SAINT.

Epistolas del glorioso doctor sant Hieronymo. Agora nueuamẽte ĩpressas. [Colophon: Sevilla, Juan Cromberger] 1541.

Collation: f°. ✠⁸, a-z⁸, ᴢ⁸, ᴣ⁸, ⅄⁸, A-E⁸; [8], ccxlvij, [1] leaves. 29cm.

Translated by Juan de Molina. Some leaves are closely trimmed at head with leaf numbers removed; leaf ccxl is mutilated with some loss of text. Ex-libris of Marga Maldonado de Sanza and Don Juan de Vernoso y Toledo.

Ref: BM; Escudero 411; Palau 292185.

110. 1542 [LÓPEZ DE AYALA, PEDRO]

Coronica del rey dõ Pedro de Castilla nueuamente impressa y emẽdada. [Colophon: Sevilla, Juan Cromberger, 18 de marzo] 1542.

Collation: f°. a-z⁸, A¹⁰; cxciiij leaves. 28.5cm.

Ref: BM; Brunet I, col. 592; Escudero 416; NUC (impf.); Palau 140776.

111. 1542 SALAYA, SANCHO DE.

Repertorio de tiẽpos nueuamente corregido por el famoso doctor Sancho de Salaya . . . el qual tambien añadio enel lunario. xxij. años sobrelo que andaua impresso hasta agora. [Colophon: Granada, 29 de abril] 1542.

Collation: 8°. a-k⁸; [80] leaves. 15cm.

Title within woodcut compartment border including the letter Y used by Sancho de Lebrija to identify his work; printer's mark of the same on verso of last leaf. — Cf. Vindel, Escudos p. 105. Ex-libris of François Florentin Achille, baron Seillière (Bibliothèque de Mello).

Ref: BM; Palau 261492.

112. 1542 LEPOLEMO (ROMANCE) SPANISH.

El libro del inuencible cauall'o Lepolemo hijo del emperador de Alemaña . . . [Colophon: Sevilla, Dominico de Robertis, 11 de agosto 1542]

Collation: f°. a-n⁸; ciiij leaves. 30cm.

Ref: Brunet III, col. 995, Escudero 494, Gallardo 825 and Palau 135976 (misnumbered 145976) describe only the De Robertis, 1548 edition.

113. 1542 [LAREDO, BERNARDINO]

Subida del monte sion nueuamente renouada . . . [Colophon: Medina del Campo, Pedro de Castro, 13 de noviembre] 1542.

Collation: 4°. ✠⁴, a-z⁸, ᴢ⁸, ᴣ⁸, ⅄⁸, A-B⁸; iiij, ccxxiiij leaves. 20cm.

Title within woodcut architectural border signed IDV (i.e. Juan de Vingles). — Cf. Nagler III, 2247; Crucifixion on leaf cxvijʳ and some of the small cuts illustrating the life of Christ signed with the same monogram. Ex-libris of Petronilla Vizó, of Carlos I, king of Portugal, and of James P. R. Lyell.

Ref: BM; Lyell p. 195, 290 and fig. 150; Palau 324284; Pérez Pastor, Medina 30.

114. 1543 NÚÑEZ DE AVENDAÑO, PEDRO.

Auiso de caçadores y de la caça. Ordenado por . . . Pero Nuñez de Auẽdaño . . . [Colophon: Alcalá de Henares, Juan de Brocar, 18 de diciembre 1543].

Collation: 8°. ✠⁴, A-E⁸; [4] xxxviij, [2] leaves. 19.5cm.

Ex-libris of James P. R. Lyell.

Ref: BM; Catalina 195; Heredia 673; HS; Lyell p. 274; NUC; Palau 197084; Salvá 2651; Souhart col. 354.

115. [CA. 1543] *Cartilla para enseñar a leer.* Seville? Dominico de Robertis? ca. 1543].

Collation: 4°. a⁸; [8] leaves. 19.5cm.

Leaves [6-8] heavily damaged, with loss of text; repairs throughout.

Ref: Lyell p. 184.

116. 1544   POZZO, PARIDE DEL.

Libro llamado batalla de dos, cōpuesto por el generoso Paris de puteo . . . que trata de batallas particulares, de reyes, emperadores, principes . . . Traduzido d'lengua toscana en nuestro vulgar castellano. Agora nueuamēte impresso . . . [Colophon: Sevilla, Dominico de Robertis, 23 de octubre 1544].

Collation: f°. A⁶, a-i⁸, k⁶; [6] lxxvij, [1] leaves (last leaf, blank, wanting). 29cm.

Full contemporary calf with unidentified arms stamped in gilt on covers. Ex-libris of James P. R. Lyell.

Ref: BM; Escudero 445; Heredia 2431; Palau 234605; Salvá 1663.

117. 1544   [VEGA, PEDRO DE LA]

La vida de nr̄o señor iesu cristo: y de su sct'issima madre: y d'los otros sct'os . . . [Colophon: Saragossa, Jorge Coci, 5 de diciembre 1544].

Collation: f°. ✠⁴, a-q⁸, r⁶, s⁶, A², t-z⁸, τ⁸, A-Z⁸, aa-ii⁸, kk⁶; [4], cxxxix, [3, the first blank], cxli-ccccxlix, [1] leaves. 37.5cm.

Also published under title: *Flos sanctorum.* The colored woodcut illus. of t.-p. (repeated uncolored on verso) and the illus. of pt.1 (Hystorias de todas las soleñidades . . . de Jesu chr̄o) are from the blocks used in Coci's Saragossa, 1521 edition (see no. 62); many of the illus. of pt.2 (Hystorias de los santos) are from the blocks used in Anton Koberger's edition of Jacobus de Varagine's *Passional,* Nuremberg, 5 Dec. 1488. — Cf. Lyell p. 135.

Ref: Lyell p. 129-40 and figs. 102-06; Palau 354946; Sánchez 243.

118. 1543 [i.e. 1544?] OCAMPO, FLORÍAN DE.

Los quatro libros primeros de la Cronica general de España que recopila el maestro Florian do canpo

. . . Zamora, [colophon: Juan Picardo, 15 de diciembre] 1543 [i.e. 1544?]. 2 copies.

Collation: f°. a-z⁸, τ⁸, aa-ff⁸, gg⁶; ccxxxv, [11] leaves (last leaf, blank, wanting in both copies).

The Harvard copies of this edition show variations: Copy A: 32cm; possibly as issued, the date in imprint at foot of t.-p. has been corrected to 1544 in a contemporary hand. In this copy, the first line of leaf xcviᵛ reads ". . . la gouernaçion y el titulo de todo lo que . . ."; the last two lines of leaf cixᵛ read ". . . pero sin menos daño que de nadie con la nasçion . . .".
Copy B: 29cm; the date on t.-p. has been corrected as in copy A; the first line of leaf xcviᵛ reads ". . . la gouernaçion y los titulos de todo lo q̄ . . ."; the last two lines of leaf cixᵛ read " . . . y mucho sin menos daño que de nadie conla naçion . . .". Leaf xciii torn, slightly affecting text; leaves closely trimmed at top, removing part of the running title and some leaf numbers.

Ref: BM; Harrisse 242; HS; NUC; Palau 198377 (mentions undated copies and copies dated 1544).

119. 1545   TOSTADO, ALONSO.

Libro intitulado Las catorze questiones del Tostado . . . [Colophon: Burgos, 20 de agosto 1545].

Collation: f°. A-J⁸, K⁴, L-Q⁸, R⁴; cxxviij leaves. 29.5cm.

Ascribed to the press of Juan de Junta: the initial P on leaf iiijᵛ is from the block used on the verso of the t.-p. in Junta's 1554 edition of *La historia d'los dos nobles caualleros* (see no. 145). Edited by Luis Ortiz, whose name appears at head of the dedication. In this copy, the 5th line of title reads ". . . a todo lo qual da sentēcia . . ."; in another Harvard copy, the 5th line of title reads ". . . a todo lo qaul [!] da sentēcia . . .".

Ref: BM; Brunet Supp. II, col. 781; Heredia 78 and 3896; HS; NUC; Palau 146767; Salvá 4022.

120. 1545   AMADIS DE GAULA. SPANISH.

. . . Los quatro libros del inuencible cauallero Amadis de gaula . . . agora nueuamente impressos. [Colophon: Medina del Campo, Juan de Villaquirán & Pedro de Castro, 1 de diciembre] 1545.

Collation: f°. a-i⁸, k⁴, l-z⁸, τ⁸, ʔ⁶, A-N⁸, O⁴, ✠⁴; cxcvi (i.e. 194), cviij, [4, the last blank] leaves. 31cm.

Numerous errors in foliation including, in 1st count, repetition of numbers cxxv and cxxxi, and omission of numbers cxxxix-cxlii. The woodcut illus. on t.-p. (mounted knight with a sword) is a close copy of that in López de Ayala's *Coronica del rey don Pedro* printed in Seville, 1542, by Juan Cromberger (see no. 110).

Ex-libris of Prince Marc-Antoine Borghesi and of James P. R. Lyell.

Ref: Brunet I, col. 208; Lyell p. 292 and fig. 228; NUC; Palau 10452; Pérez Pastor, Medina 44.

121. 1545 [PULGAR, HERNANDO DEL]

Habes in hoc volvmine amice lector. Aelii Antonii Nebrissensis Rervm a Fernando & Elisabe Hispaniarū foelicissimis regibus gesta decades duas . . . [Colophon at end of pt. 1: Granada] 1545. 2 copies.

Collation: f°. 3pts. in 1v. Copy A: 34.5cm; copy B: 32cm.
Pt. 1: A^8, B-P^6, Q^2; [8], lxxxvi leaves.
Pt. 2: ✠^{4}, a-v^6, x^2; [4], cxxiiii (i.e. 122) leaves.
Pt. 3: π^2, aa-nn^6; [2], lxxvii, [1] leaves.

Each pt. has special t.-p.; titles within woodcut ornamental border including the letter Y used by the editor and printer Sancho de Lebrija to identify his work; his printer's mark appears at end of pts. 1 and 3. — Cf. Vindel, Escudos p. 105; leaf ccxxii of pt. 2 misnumbered cxxiiii. Pt. 1 is a Latin translation by Antonio de Lebrija of Hernando del Pulgar's *Historia de los reyes catolicos* and Luis Correa's *Historia de la guerra de Navarra*; pt. 2 contains *Rervm in Hispania gestarum chronicon* by Rodrigo Ximénes de Rada and *Genealogia regum Hispanorum* by Alfonso de Cartagena; pt. 3, the *Paralipomenon Hispaniae* of Joan de Margarit i Pau. Ex-libris of Eugene, prince of Savoy (copy B).

Ref: BM; Lyell p. 254-56 and fig. 202-03; NUC; Palau 189342, 242126 and 377242.

122. 1546 ALCALÁ, LUIS DE.

Tractado d'los prestamos que passan entre mercaderes y tractantes . . . Compuesto por fray Luys d' Alcala . . . Segunda vez impresso . . . [Colophon: Toledo, Juan de Ayala, 2 de julio] 1546.

Collation: 4°. ✠^{4}, a-f^8, g^4; [4], lij leaves. 20.5cm.

Ex-libris of the Biblioteca Heberiana and of Sir William Sterling-Maxwell.

Ref: BM; NUC; Palau 5690; Pérez Pastor, Toledo 208.

123. 1546 BIDPAI. SPANISH.

Exemplario. Libro llamado Exemplario: en el qual se cõtiene muy buena doctrina y graues sentencias debaxo de graciosas fabulas. [Colophon: Sevilla, Jacome Cromberger, 1546].

Collation: f°. a-f^8, g-h^6; lx leaves. 27cm.

The woodcut illustrative material is for the most part from the blocks used in the Seville, 1534 edition. — Cf. Heredia 2420.

Ex-libris of James P. R. Lyell.

Ref: Lyell p. 172; NUC; Palau 85007; not in Escudero.

124. [1546] [GÓMEZ DE CASTRO, ALVARO]

Pvblica laetitia, qva dominvs Ioannes Martinus Silicaeus archiepiscopus toletanus ab Schola complutẽsi susceptus est . . . [Colophon: Alcalá de Henares, Juan de Brocar] [1546].

Collation: 4°. a^4, A-H^8, I^6; [4] leaves, 137, [1] pages, [1] leaf. 22cm.

Ex-libris of Richard Heber and of James P. R. Lyell.

Ref: BM [1546?]; Catalina 213; Lyell p. 274-76 and fig. 218; Palau 103900.

125. 1547 MANDEVILLE, SIR JOHN.

. . . Libro de las maravillas del mũdo llamado Selua deleytosa, que trata del viaje de la tierra santa de Hierusalem . . . q̃ escriuio el noble cauallero Juan de mandauilla . . . agora de nueuo impresso corregido y emẽdado. [Colophon: Alcalá de Henares, 28 de marzo] 1547.

Collation: f°. ✠^{2}, a-i^6, k^4; [2], lvij, [1] leaves. 28cm.

Many of the woodcut illus. are copied from those of the Augsburg 1481 edition published by Anton Sorg. — Cf. Albert Schramm's *Der Bilderschmuck der Fruhdrucke 4. Die Drucke von Anton Sorg in Augsburg.* Leipzig, 1921, nos. 579-700. Leaf at end (containing colophon) wanting, here supplied in modern facsimile.

Ref: BM; Palau 148357; not in Catalina.

126. 1547 DIAZ TANCO DE FREJENAL, VASCO.

Libro intitulado Palinodia, de la nephanda y fiera nacion de los turcos, y de su engañoso arte y cruel modo de guerrear . . . Recopilado por Vasco diaz tanco . . . [Colophon: Orense, Vasco Diaz Tanco de Frejenal, 15 de setiembre] 1547.

Collation: f°. π^1, ✠^{8}, (✠$8+\chi 1$), a-d^8, e^6, f-g^8, h^6; [11], ii-viij, xj-lxij leaves. 30cm.

Device of author-printer on verso of last leaf. Leaves b1-4 missigned bij-v. Tears and repairs in margins; wormholes throughout, slightly affecting text. The Mayans Gohier copy with the ex-libris of the Biblioteca de Salvá, of Ricardo Heredia and of William Inglis Morse.

Ref: BM; Brunet II, col. 679; Heredia 3264 and fig.; HS; NUC; Palau 72902; Rodriguez Moñino 9; Salvá 3310.

127. 1547 CARBONELL, PEDRO MIGUEL.

Chroniques de Espãya fins aci no diuulgades: que tracta d'ls nobles e' inuictissims reys dels Gots . . . Compilada per . . . Pere Miquel Carbonell . . . [Colophon: Barcelona, Carles Amoros, 15 de noembre 1546] Nouament imprimida en lany. 1547.

Collation: f°. ✠^{4}, a-d^8, e^{10}, f-z^8, A-H^8, J^{10}; [4], xxxii, xxxii-lxxviii, lxxviii-cclvii, [1] leaves. 29cm.

Leaf cxxv, misnumbered cxxi in this copy, is correctly numbered in another Harvard copy.

Ref: Aguiló 2815; BM; HS; NUC; Palau 43729; Salvá 2855.

128. 1548 MENA, JUAN DE.

Copilacion d'todas las obras del famosissimo poeta Juã de mena: cõuiene saber Las. ccc. cõ otras. xxiiij coplas y su glosa. y la Coronacion delas coplas delos siete peccados mortales: con otras cartas y coplas y canciones suyas. Agora nueuamente añadidas ʒ imprimidas. [Colophon on leaf xxvj^v (2d count): Toledo, en casa de Fernando de Sancta Catalina defunto, 15 de diciembre 1547] 1548.

Collation: f°. a-n^8; A-B^8, C^{10}; ciiij; xxvj leaves. 29cm.

"La coronacion . . . Con otras coplas agora nueuamente añadidas a la fin (xxvj leaves, 2d count) has special t.-p. dated 1548.

Ref: BM (with colophon dated 1546 [!]); HS; NUC; Pérez Pastor, Toledo 228; Salvá 792, note.

129. 1548 CATHOLIC CHURCH. LITURGY AND RITUAL. MISSAL.

Missale romanum. [Colophon: Saragossa, 1548].

Collation: f°. ✠^{10}, a-z^8, A-G^8, H^{10}; [10], ccxlix, [1, blank] leaves. 20.5cm.

The woodcut illus. on t.-p. (St. Jerome and the lion) is from the same block as in Coci's 1511 edition (see no. 26); the compartment border includes, at foot, the joint monogram of Pedro Bernuz and Bartholomé de Nagera, successors to the Coci press; some of the woodcut illus. are from the blocks used in Bernhard von Breydenbach's *Viaje de la tierra sancta*, Saragossa, 1498 and Pedro de la Vega's *Flos Sanctorum*, Saragossa, 1521 (see no. 62). — Cf. Lyell p. 140 and fig. 107. In this copy, the last line of colophon reads ". . . Cesarauguste . . ."; as described in Palau 173060, it reads "Cesaraugustae (sic)". Ex-libris of George Dunn and of James P. R. Lyell.

Ref: Sánchez 280; Vindel, Man. 1766a.

130. 1549 SPAIN. LAWS, STATUTES, ETC., 1516-1556 (CHARLES I)

Las pregmaticas y capitulos que su .M. d'l emperador y rey nño señor hizo en las cortes q̃ se touierõ con el serenissimo principe don Phelipe nño señor, en su nombre. En Valladolid. Año d'. M.D. xlviij. . . . [Colophon: Valladolid, Francisco Fernandez de Cordova, 3 de febrero 1549].

Collation: f°. A-G^8, H^6; lxii leaves. 30.5cm.

Signature H (leaves lvii-lxii) wanting in this copy.

Ref: Alcocer 150; Jesús F. Martínez Elorza. *Orígenes y estado actual de la biblioteca del Instituto de Jovellanos.* Gijón, 1902, p. 81 (g); NUC; Palau 235095; Salvá 3650.

131. 1549 GUEVARA, ANTONIO DE.

Libro primero [-Segunda parte] d' las epistolas familiares del reuerendissimo señor don Antonio de Gueuara . . . [Colophons: Valladolid, Juan de Villaquirán, 9 de marzo; Sebastián Martinez, 8 de julio] 1549.

Collation: f°. 2 pts. in 1v. 29cm.
Pt.1: π^2, A-0^8, P^6; cxx leaves.
Pt.2: A^{10}, B-H^8, J^{12}, K-N^8, O^6; cxviij (i.e. 116) leaves.

Titles within ornamental border including at foot the initials SM [i.e. Sebastían Martínez, the publisher]. In pt. 1, on leaf xcix, there is a small cancel slip reading "N" pasted over the erroneous signature ("M"); leaf [ii] (tabla) is misbound after leaf x. Ms. note at foot of t.-p., dated 24 April 1585, in the hand of the Arandan censor Fray Gonzalo. In pt. 2, numbers ix and x are repeated in foliation and leaf cxiv is misnumbered cxviij.

Ref: BM; R. Foulché-Delbosc. "Bibliographie espagnole de Fray Antonio de Guevara," no. 46, in *Revue Hispanique*, XXXIII, 84, 1915; NUC; Palau 110213.

132. 1549   ORTIZ, BLAS.

Svmmi templi Toletani perq3 graphica descriptio; Blasio Ortizio . . . autore. [Colophon: Toledo, Juan de Ayala, March] 1549.

Collation: 8°. a-v⁸; cxljx, [11] leaves (last two leaves blank, the second wanting). 15cm.

With a preface by Alfonso Cedillo.

Ref: BM; NUC; Palau 205597; Pérez Pastor, Toledo 238.

133. 1549   GREGORIUS I, THE GREAT, SAINT, POPE.

. . . Los morales de sant Gregorio papa: doctor de la santa yglesia. [Colophon at end of v. 2: Sevilla, Juan Varela de Salamanca, 8 de junio 1549].

Collation: f°. 2v. 31cm.
V. 1: S¹⁰, a-z⁸, &⁸, aa-dd⁸, ee⁶; [10], ccxxx leaves. 31cm.
V. 2 wanting; colophon transcribed from Palau 290990.

The Crucifixion on verso of t.-p. in v. 1 is from the block used in the Juan de Varela, Granada, 1504 edition of Guillaume Durand's *Rationale divinorum officiorum* (see no. 9). Translated from the Latin by Alonso Alvarez de Toledo. Full contemporary blind-tooled black morocco.

Ref: Escudero 507.

134. 1549   *La cronica del rey dõ Rodrigo* con la destruycion de España, y como los moros la ganaron. Nueuamente corregida . . . Toledo, Juan Ferrer, [colophon: 20 de julio] 1549.

Collation: f°. a-z⁸, A⁸, B-C⁶, A⁸; cciij, [9, the first blank] leaves. 30.5cm.

Generally attributed to Pedro del Corral. — Cf. Norton 803.

Ex-libris of the Biblioteca de Salvá and of Ricardo Heredia.

Ref: Brunet I, col. 1881; Heredia 3116; Palau 65008; Pérez Pastor, Toledo 235; Salvá 1584.

135. 1549   [SAGREDO, DIEGO DE]

Medidas del romano ǫ Vitruuio nueuamẽte impresas z añadidas muchas pieças . . . [Colophon: Toledo, Juan de Ayala, diciembre] 1549.

Collation: 4°. a-d⁸, e¹²; [44, the last blank] leaves. 21cm.

Author named on [1]ᵛ.

Ref: Brunet V, col. 31; Palau 284926; Pérez Pastor, Toledo 240.

136. 1549   SPAIN. LAWS, STATUTES, ETC., 1516-1556 (CHARLES I)

Las cortes de Valladolid. del anno .M.D.XL.VIII. Las pregmaticas y capitulos que su magestad del emperador y rey nuestro señor hizo en las cortes que se touieron con el serenissimo principe don Phelippe nuestro señor, en su nombre. En Valladolid. Año de mill y quinientos quaranta y ocho. Van añadidas las pregmaticas de los arrendadores del pan . . . [Colophon: Valladolid, Francisco Fernandez de Cordova, diciembre 1549].

Collation: f°. A-G⁸; lv, [1] leaves (last leaf, blank, wanting). 29.5cm.

Leaves xi and xiv (B3.6) wanting in this copy.

Ref: Palau 63147.

137. 1550   [ESCOBAR, LUIS DE]

Las quatrocientas respuestas a otras tantas preguntas . . . Con quinientos prouerbios de consejos y auisos . . . agora segunda vez estãpadas, corregidas y emendadas . . . [Colophon: Valladolid, Francisco Fernandez de Cordova, 25 de mayo 1550].

Collation: f°. A-B⁸, C¹⁰, D-X⁸, Y-Z⁶; clxxxij leaves. 28.5cm.

The author's name appears in an acrostic on leaf cxxxvᵛ.

Ex-libris of James P. R. Lyell.

Ref: Alcocer 158; BM; HS (impf.); Heredia 2749; NUC; Palau 81068; Salvá 2065.

138. 1550   [BURGOS, PEDRO ALFONSO DE]

Libro dela historia y milagros hechos a inuocacion de nuestra Señora de Montserrat. [Colophon: Barcelona, Pedro Mompezat] 1550.

Collation: 4°. π⁴, A-BB⁸, CC⁶, A⁸, B²; [4], 206, [10] leaves (last leaf, blank, wanting). 21.5cm.

Sometimes ascribed to Gonzalo de Sojo. — Cf. Lyell p. 151. As in Gallardo 947, the first four leaves at front of this copy are printed in the same type as the nine leaves of Tabla at end; the latter have special imprint: Excudebat Barcinone Petrus Botin. 1550. The Heber, Richard Ford and Huth copy with the ex-libris of T.v Freundtsperg and of James P. R. Lyell.

Ref: Lyell p. 151-54 with fig.; Palau 37329.

139. 1551   [VEGA, PEDRO DE LA]

La vida de nr̃o señor jesu cristo: y de su sanctissima madre, y delos otros sanctos . . . Agora de nuevo añadidas algunas vidas de sanctos . . . Saragossa, Bartholomé de Nagera, 1551.

Collation: f°. π⁴, a-q⁸, r⁶, s⁴; [4], cxxxviii leaves. 35.5cm.

The woodcut illus. on t.-p. (printed in red, green, brown and yellow) and some of the illus. are from the blocks used in the 1521 and 1544 Coci editions (see nos. 62 and 117); others are signed IDV (i.e. Juan de Vingles). — Cf. Nagler III, 2247.
Fore-edge and lower margin of t.-p. repaired, affecting border; some of the leaves are mounted on stubs.

Ref: Palau 354948; Vindel, Man. 3095 (this copy) gives date as 1541 [!].

140. 1552   [ESCOBAR, LUIS DE]

La segvnda parte de las quatrocientas respuestas. en q̃ se contienen otras quatrocientas respuestas a otras tantas preguntas . . . Valladolid, Francisco Fernandez de Cordova, [colophon: 2 de enero] 1552.

Collation: f°. A¹⁰, B-Z⁸, aa-gg⁸, hh⁶; [2] ccxlv, [1, blank] leaves. 27.5cm.

The woodcut illus. on t.-p. (arms of the dedicatee, Fadrique Enríquez) is from the block used in the Valladolid, 1550 edition of the 1st part (see no. 137).

Leaves closely trimmed, removing part of the side notes and leaf numbers.

Ref: Alcocer 179; BM; Heredia 2750 and fig.; HS; NUC; Palau 81069; Salvá 2066.

141. 1552   DIAZ TANCO DE FREJENAL, VASCO.

Jardin del alma xp̃iana do se tractã las significaciones d'la missa y delas horas canonicas . . . recopilado por el maestro. v. d. Frexenal . . . [Colophon: Valladolid, Juan de Carvajal, 1 de febrero 1552].

Collation: 4°. A⁴, B¹², C-R⁸; cxxxv, [1] leaves. 20cm.

Title within compartment border incorporating a device used earlier by the printer Pedro de Castro. Some copies have a typographic ornament in place of Castro's device. — Cf. Vindel, Escudos no. 135 and p. 155, note. In this copy, the t.-p. is transposed in binding with leaf [C]1, a divisional title beginning "Jardin d'l alma xp̃iana para clerigos y frayles . . .".

Ref: BM; HS; NUC; Palau 72905; Rodrigues-Moñino 10; Salvá 3881; Vindel, Man. 828a-b (this copy, with reprod. of divisional t.-p. erroneously thought to be the t.-p.); not in Alcocer.

142. 1552   ORTIZ, FRANCISCO.

Epistolas familiares del mvy reuerendo padre fray francisco Ortiz . . . Contienen se juntamente en este volumẽ algunas otras obras del mesmo padre . . . [Colophon: Alcalá de Henares, Juan de Brocar, 19 de noviembre 1551] 1552.

Collation: f°. ¶⁴, A-M⁸, N¹⁰; [4], cv, [1, blank] leaves. 29cm.

Full contemporary blind-tooled black morocco, wormed.

Ref: BM; Catalina 250; HS; NUC; Palau 205626.

143. 1552   XENOPHON. SPANISH. GRACIAN.

Las obras de Xenophon trasladadas de griego en castellano por el secretario Diego Gracian, diuididas en tres partes . . . [Colophon: Salamanca, Juan de Junta] 1552.

Collation: f°. ✠⁸, A-Z⁸, a-e⁸; [8], 222, [2] leaves. 29.5cm.

Printed at foot of t.-p.: Esta tassado en [inserted in ms.: 298] marauedis. Ex-libris of the Biblioteca de Salvá and of Ricardo Heredia.

Ref: BM; Heredia 2984; HS; NUC; Palha 2695; Palau 376843; Salvá 2799.

144. 1553   [CUEVA, GASPAR MIGUEL DE
              LA]

. . . Historia del misterio diuino del sanctissimo sacramento del altar q̃ esta enlos corporales de Daroca . . . [Colophon: Alcalá de Henares, Juan de Brocar, 20 de mayo 1553].

Collation: 4°. A-L⁴, M⁶; [4], xlv, [1] leaves. 19cm.

Author named on A2ʳ. Full contemporary red morocco with unidentified ecclesiastical arms stamped in gilt and enameled on covers; gauffered edges.

Ref: BM; P. Benigno Fernández. *Impresos de Alcalá en la Biblioteca del Escorial.* Madrid, 1913, 90; Catalina 258; R. Esteban Abad. *Estudio historico-politico sobre la ciudad y comunidad de Daroca.* Teruel, 1959, XLV and fig.; NUC; Palau 66141, note.

145. 1554   OLIVIER DE CASTILLE
              (ROMANCE) SPANISH. 1554.

La historia d'los dos nobles caualleros Oliueros de castilla y Artus de Algarue. [Colophon: Burgos, Juan de Junta] 1554.

Collation: 4°. A-H⁸, J⁴; [68, the last blank] leaves. 20cm.

Lower corner of J3 repaired with some of the text strengthened in ms. Full contemporary calf with arms (of the Castillo de Retuerto family?) stamped in gilt on covers. Ex-libris of James P. R. Lyell.

Ref: Lyell p. 201-04 and fig. 160; Palau 200855.

146. [1554?]   SEVILLE. ORDINANCES, ETC.

Estas son las ordenãças de los sastres y calceteros y jubeteros de esta cibdad de Seuilla . . . [Sevilla, 1554?]

Collation: f°. a-f²; [12] leaves. 29cm.

Ordinances dated Friday April 20, 1554, on a2ʳ. Ascribed to the press of Martin de Montesdoca, whose mark, in the 1554 edition of Miguel de Fuenllana's *Libro de musica para vihuela,* is signed BDS as is the title vignette of this edition. Printed on vellum. With ms. annotations and corrections throughout, and the following ms. inscription at end: Yo el dicho

Juan Cataño las hize enprimiri y las correicon el [trimmed]nal y fiz aqui este mio signo en testimonio de v[erdad] Juan Cataño. Full contemporary red morocco with royal arms of Spain stamped in gilt on covers.

Ref: Lyell p. 180-81 and fig. 139; not in Escudero.

147. 1557   IRUROZQUI, PEDRO.

Series totivs historiae sacri Euangelii, Iesv Christi, quae quatuor Euangelistis concinnata . . . autore Petro Irurozqui . . . Estella, Adrián de Anvers, [colophon: 5 December] 1557.

Collation: f°. 5pts. in 1v. 31.5cm.

Pt. 1: ✠⁶, A-I⁴; [6], xxi, xxi-xxxiv, [1] leaves (last leaf, presumably blank, wanting).
Pt.2: AA², BB-HH⁴; [2], xxviii leaves.
Pt.3: AAA², BBB-LLL⁴; [2], xl leaves.
Pts.4 & 5: AAAA-ZZZZ⁴, &&&&⁶; [4], lxiiii leaves; xxix, [1] leaves.

Each part with special t.-p. The erroneous signatures FFFF and FFFFij on leaves xxi and xxii of pt.4 are covered with paste-on slips bearing the correct signatures, i.e. GGGG and GGGGij.

Ref: Palau 121530; Pérez Goyena 55.

148. 1561   SALAMANCA, SPAIN.
              UNIVERSIDAD.

Estatvtos hechos por la mvy insigne vniversidad de Salamanca. Año M.D.LXI. Salamanca, Juan Maria de Terranova, 1561.

Collation: f°. A-I⁸, K⁴, A⁶; 75, [7] leaves. 30.5cm.

Bound with the *Constitvtiones,* 1562 and the *Priuilegios,* [1561?] (See nos. 151 and 149).

Ref: NUC; Palau 83538, note.

149. [1561?]   SALAMANCA, SPAIN.
                UNIVERSIDAD.

Los priuilegios que esta muy insigne vniuersidad de Salamanca tiene concedidos de los reyes de España . . . [Salamanca, 1561?]

Collation: f°. A²; [2] leaves. 30.5cm.

Ascribed to the press of Juan Maria de Terranova (the woodcut initial E flanked by two small angels is commonly used by Terranova). Bound with the *Constitvtiones,* 1562 and the *Estatvtos,* 1561 (see nos. 151 and 148).

Ref: NUC; Palau 83538, note.

150. 1562 CATHOLIC CHURCH. LITURGY
AND RITUAL. PASSIONARIUM.

Passionarium oxomense nouiter excussum . . . Bur-
go de Osma, Diego Fernandez de Cordova, 1562.

Collation: f°. a-l⁸; lxxxviij leaves. 36cm.

Full contemporary blind-tooled calf. Ex-libris of
Tomas Paz and of the Monastery of Sta. Catalina de
Sena de Valladolid.

Ref: Palau 214429.

151. 1562 SALAMANCA, SPAIN.
UNIVERSIDAD.

Constitvtiones tam commodae aptaeqve, qvam
sanctae almae Salmanticencis academiae toto terra-
rum orbe florentissimae. Salamanca, Juan Maria de
Terranova, 1562

Collation: f°. ¶⁸, A-C⁸, D⁴; [8], 28 leaves. 30.5cm.

With this are bound the *Estatvtos,* 1561, and the *Priuilegios,* [1561?] (see nos. 148 and 149). Full contemporary blind-stamped calf, rebacked. Ex-libris of the
Marques de Astorga.

Ref: NUC; Palau 59852.

152. 1563 HERRERA, GABRIEL ALONSO DE.

Libro de agricultura que es de la labrança y criança
. . . Copilado por Gabriel Alonso de Herrera . . .
Nueuamente corregido y añadido por el mesmo
. . . Valladolid, Francisco Fernandez de Cordova,
[colophon: 8 de agosto] 1563.

Collation: f°. A⁶, B-Z⁸, ⲍ⁸, a-c⁸; vi, ix-ccxvj leaves.
29cm.

Tear in lower margin of t.-p., slightly affecting
woodcut border.

Ref: Alcocer 235; BM; Gallardo 2498; Heredia 459:
NUC (this copy only); Palau 114096, note; Palha 444;
Salvá 2575.

153. 1563 SERLIO, SEBASTIANO.

Tercero y qvarto libro de architectura de Sebastian
serlio boloñes . . . Traduzido đ toscano en lengua
castellana, por Francisco de Villalpando, architecto
. . . Toledo [colophons: Juan de Ayala] 1563.

Collation: f°. 2 pts. in 1v. 34cm.

Pt.3: π¹, A-V⁴; [1], lxxx leaves.
Pt.4: A-T⁴; [1] leaf, ii-v pages, vi-lxxviii leaves.
Each part with special t.-p. and separate colophon.
Title-page of Pt.4 wanting.

Ref: HS; NUC; Palau 309580; Pérez Pastor, Toledo
297.

154. 1564 MEXÍA, PEDRO.

Hystoria imperial y cesarea: enla qual en summa se
contienē las vidas y hechos de todos los cesares
emperadores de Roma . . . La qual compuso y
ordeno . . . Pero Mexia . . . Agora en esta vltima
impression nueuamente emendada y corregida.
[Colophon: Sevilla, Sebastian Trujillo, 25 de agosto]
1564.

Collation: f°. ✠⁶, A-SS⁸, TT⁶; [6], cccxxxiiij leaves.
33cm.

Tear in leaf vi, slightly affecting text.

Ref: Escudero 615; Palau 167345.

155. 1564 LÓPEZ DE MENDOZA, IÑIGO, 4.
DUQUE DEL INFANTADO.

Memorial de cosas notables, compuesto por don
Yñigo Lopez de Mendoça . . . Guadalajara, Pedro
de Robles y Francisco de Cormellas, [colophon: 16
de setiembre] 1564.

Collation: f°. π², A-Ii⁸; [11] leaves, 454 pages, [20,
the last blank] leaves. 30.5cm.

Gallardo 2770 calls for a frontispiece not present in
this copy or in any of the references cited below.

Ref: BM; Juan Catalina García. *Biblioteca de escritores
de la provincia de Guadalajara.* Madrid, 1899, no. 633;
Heredia 8298; HS ; Palau 141458; Salvá 2769.

156. 1564 LISUARTE DE GRECIA. SPANISH.

. . .El septimo libro de Amadis, en el qual se trata
de los grandes hechos en armas de Lisuarte de Grecia
hijo de Esplādian. y de los grandes hechos de Perion
de Gaula . . . Estella, Adrián de Anvers, 1564.

Collation: f°. A-T⁶; cxiij, [1] leaves (last leaf, presumably blank, wanting). 29cm.

Ex-libris of James P. R. Lyell.

Ref: Palau 10485; Pérez Goyena 72; Salvá 1514, note.

157. 1565 [LA MARCHE, OLIVIER DE]

El cavallero determinado tradvzido de lengua frācesa en castellana por don Hernando de Acuña . . . Barcelona, Claudio Bornat, 1565.

Collation: 4°. A-O⁸, P⁶; 118 leaves. 18cm.

The woodcut title vignette (imperial arms of Charles V) is from the block used in the Antwerp, 1555 edition; the full-page woodcut illus. by Arnold Nicolaï (sometimes wrongly ascribed to Juan de Arfe y Villafañe. — Cf. Nagler 81) are from the blocks used in the Antwerp 1553 and 1555 editions; the one on leaf [72] with figure of Plazo in foreground cut down to proportionate size (43mm), is in second state as in the 1555 edition. — Cf. Peeters-Fontainas p. 189-90. The translation is Acuña's adaptation into Spanish verse of a prose translation by Charles V. Ex-libris of the Biblioteca de Salvá and of Ricardo Heredia.

Ref: BM; Gallardo 33; Heredia 2106; HS; NUC; Palau 130351; Salvá 1628.

158. 1569 GÓMEZ DE CASTRO, ALVARO.

De rebvs gestis a Francisco Ximenio, Cisnerio, archiepiscopo toletano, libri octo. Aluaro Gomecio toletano authore . . . Alcalá de Henares, Andre de Angulo, 1569.

Collation: f°. ¶⁸, *⁸, A-Gg⁸; [16], 240 leaves. 30cm.

Ref: BN; BM; Catalina 439; HS; NUC; Palau 103905.

159. 1569 MEJÍA Y PONCE DE LEÓN, LUIS.

Λακονισμος. Laconismvs, sev Chilonivm pro pragmaticae qvu panis preciū taxatur in interioris foro hominis elucidatione, Lvdovico Messiae . . . autore . . . Seville, Juan Gutierrez, 1569.

Collation: f°. A-S⁸, T⁴, V-X⁸, Y⁶ (Y6 = plate); 170 (i.e. 169) leaves, [1] leaf of plates. 29.5cm.

Number 149 omitted in foliation.

Ref: Escudero 629; HS; NUC; Palau 160006.

160. 1572 AGUILAR, PEDRO DE.

Tractado de la cavalleria de la gin[e]ta cōpuesto y ordenado, por el capitā Pedro de Agu[i]lar . . . Acabose de cōponer por el mes de março de. 1570. siendo el auctor, de edad de cinquēta y cinco años . . . Sevilla, Hernando Diaz, [colophon: 28 de febrero] 1572.

Collation: 4°. *⁴, A-Y⁴; [4], 84, [4] leaves. 19.5cm.

Title-page and some lower margins mutilated and repaired, affecting title and text. Ex-libris of M.G. and of T. Norton.

Ref: Escudero 657; Heredia 647; Palau 3625; Salvá 2597.

161. 1572 ARFE Y VILLAFAÑE, JUAN DE.

Qvilatador de la plata, oro, y piedras, compvesto por Ioan Arphe de Villafañe . . . Valladolid, Alonso y Diego Fernandez de Cordova, 1572.

Collation: 4°. ¶⁴, A-I⁸; [4], 71, [1] leaves. 20cm.

Signed in ms., at foot of the last page: Arphe. Ex-libris of the Museo del Montino and of Joseph J. Cooke.

Ref: Alcocer 271: BM; Heredia 4352; NUC; Palau 16053; Salvá 2553 (lleva al fin un autógrafo de Arfe).

162. 1572 [VEGA, PEDRO DE LA]

Flos sanctorvm. La vida de Nvestro señor Iesv Christo, y de sv sanctissima madre. Y de los otros sanctos, segun la orden de sus fiestas. Ahora de nueuo corregido y emmendado, por el . . . doctor Gonçalo Millan. Y añadido de algunas vidas de sanctos . . . Sevilla, Juan Gutierrez, 1572.

Collation: f°. (!)⁶, B-E⁸, f-g⁸, H-K⁸, L⁶, M-P⁸, Q⁶, R-T⁸, U-X⁶, a-z⁸, Aa-Ll⁸, MM-YY⁸, ZZ⁶, aaa⁶; [6], clxxxiiij (i.e. 152), ccclxij (i.e. 372) leaves. 36cm.

Numerous errors in foliation. Some of the woodcut illus. are signed ADCF. Tear in leaves ccv and ccl (2d count), slightly affecting text; occasional repairs in margins.

Ref: BM; Lyell p. 196 and fig. 152 (refers to the *Pasionario* printed by Matias Gast in Salamanca, 1570, with illustrations also signed ADCF); NUC (microfilm of BM copy); Palau 354952; not in Escudero.

163. 1573 [LA MARCHE, OLIVIER DE]

El cavallero determinado, traduzido de lengua francesa en castellana, por don Hernando de Acuña . . . Salamanca, Pedro Laso, 1573.

Collation: 4°. A-P⁸; 118, [2] leaves. 19cm.

The full-page woodcut illus. by Arnold Nicolaï are from the blocks used in the Antwerp, 1553 and 1555 editions and in the Barcelona, 1565 edition (see no. 157). The translation is Hernando de Acuña's adaptation into Spanish verse of a prose translation by Charles V. Leaves 117-18 wanting; [1]st unnumbered leaf at end (P7), containing license to print, misbound before t.-p.

Ref: HS; NUC; Palau 130353; Peeters-Fontainas p. 190-91.

164. 1576 [*Abededario*] ✠A a b c . . . [Colophon: Toledo, Francisco de Guzmán, 1576].

Collation: 8°. a⁸; [8] leaves. 16cm.

Apparently unrecorded.

165. 1576 CATHOLIC CHURCH. LITURGY AND RITUAL. PASSIONARIUM.

Passionarivm cum officio maioris hebdomadę iuxta formam missalis & breuiarij romani . . . Ioannis Roderici de Villamaior . . . industria & labore recognitum. Toledo, Juan de Plaça, 1576.

Collation: f°. π², ✠⁴, ℂ⁶, a-i⁶, l⁶, m⁴, n-r⁶, s-t⁴, v-z⁶, Aa-Ii⁶, Ll-Mm⁶, Nn⁴; [208] leaves. 35cm.

In some copies the t.-p. is printed in black; this copy has the title printed in black and red and has a cancel slip pasted on the lowest staff of leaf c1ʳ. Tears in leaves f3, n4 and Cc6, slightly affecting text and music.

Ref: BM; Palau 214435; Pérez Pastor, Toledo 343.

166. 1577 ORDEN MILITAR DE SANTIAGO.

La regla y stablescimientos de la cavalleria de Sanctiago del Espada . . . [Colophon: Madrid, Francisco Sanchez, 1577]. 2 copies.

Collation: π⁴ (π2.3 = plates), A-B⁶, A-CC⁶; [14], 156 leaves, [2] leaves of plates.

Title within architectural border, and woodcut arms of the order within scroll border by Antonio de Arfe; woodcut equestrian figure within full page architectural border.
Copy A: 30cm; leaf [14] contains the errata on the recto and the verso is blank; leaf 72 is misnumbered 62 and leaf 109 is unsigned. Full contemporary black morocco gilt-tooled in a fan design. Ex-libris of S.C., and of W. Vernon. One of the plates (equestrian figure) is wanting.
Copy B: 32cm; leaf [14] contains the approbation on

the recto and the errata on verso; leaf 72 is rightly numbered and leaf 109 is signed T. Full contemporary black morocco gilt-tooled in a shell design, edges gilt.

Ref: NUC (impf.); Palau 253974; Pérez Pastor, Madrid 116; Walters Art Gallery, Baltimore. *The history of bookbinding 525-1950 A.D., an exhibition held at the Baltimore Museum of Art, Nov. 12, 1957 to Jan. 12, 1958.* Baltimore, 1957, 246 (copy A).

167. 1580 GONZALEZ DE LA TORRE, JUAN.

Dialogo llamado Nvncio legato mortal, en metros redondos castellanos . . . Compuesto por Iuan Gonçalez de la Torre . . . Madrid, Francisco Sanchez, 1580 [colophon: 1570 [!]].

Collation: 8°. A⁸ (A1 + 1) B-N⁸, O²; 105, [2] leaves. 15.5cm.

The printer's mark on verso of the last leaf is a reduced copy (without initials) of that used by Martin de Montesdoca in his Seville, 1554 edition of Luis de Miranda's *Comedia prodiga.* — Cf. Salvá 1320. Ex-libris of S.C., and of Sir William Sterling-Maxwell.

Ref: Heredia 5476, HS, Palau 105999, Pérez Pastor, Madrid 153, Salvá 653, none mentioning the colophon dated 1570 [!].

168. 1582 ARGOTE DE MOLINA GONZALO, ASCRIBED AUTHOR.

Libro, de la monteria qve mando escrevir el mvy alto y mvy poderoso rey don Alonso de Castilla, y de Leon, vltimo deste nombre. Acrecentado por Gonçalo Argote de Molina . . . Sevilla, Andrea Pescioni, 1582.

Collation: f°. (?)⁶, A⁶, B-L⁸, M⁶, ¶⁸, ¶¶-¶¶¶⁶, ¶¶¶¶⁴; [6], 91, [1, blank], 25 (i.e. 23), [1] leaves. 30cm.

Numbers 15 and 16 (2d count) omitted in foliation. Generally attributed to Argote de Molina; sometimes ascribed to Alfonso X. — Cf. Palau 16167. In this copy the "Discvrso" (25 (i.e.. 23) leaves), usually found at end, is bound at front before the "Libro, de la monteria" (91 leaves). Ex-libris of Schwerdt, of Joachim Manín y Mendozas, of the Biblioteca de Salvá and of Ricardo Heredia.

Ref: BM; Brunet I, col. 420; Escudero 726; Heredia 675; HS; NUC; A. P. Chaguaceda. *El historiador G. Argote de Molina.* Madrid, 1949, p. 62; Salvá 2635; Souhart col. 24; not in Lyell.

169. 1582 GÓMEZ MIEDES, BERNARDINO.

Bernardini Gomesii Miedis . . . de vita & rebus gestis Iacobi I. regis Aragonum, cognomento expugnatoris. Libri. XX . . . Valencia, widow of Pedro de Huete, 1582.

Collation: f°. ¶⁴, A-AA⁸, BB⁶, CC¹⁰; [4] leaves, 394 pages, [11] leaves (least leaf, blank, wanting). [1] leaf of plates. 29cm.

Ref: BM; HS; NUC; Palau 104101; Salvá 2965; not in Serrano.

170. 1585 PEGUERA, LUIS DE.

Liber qvaestionvm criminalivm in actv practico . . . Authore don Ludouico à Peguera . . . Cvm summarijs & indice locupletissimo . . . Barcelona, Hubert Gotart, 1585.

Collation: f°. ¶⁸, A-Q⁶, R⁴, a⁶, b⁸; [8], 98, [16, the first two blank] leaves. 30cm.

Ex-libris of Charles Howard, baron Effingham, and of the Royal Society of London (ex dono Henry Howard, duke of Norfolk).

Ref: BM; NUC; Palau 216338 (Liber quaestiones [!] criminalium . . .).

171. 1586 [i.e. 1587] AGUILÓN, PEDRO DE.

El secretario Agvilon. Historia del dvqve Carlos de Borgoña, bisaguelo del emperador Carlos Quinto. Pamplona, Thomas Porralis, 1586 [colophon: al fin del mes de abril 1587].

Collation: 4°. A-N⁸, O⁴, (O4 = plate); [4] leaves, 205, [1] pages, [1] leaf of plates. 22cm.

Adapted in part from *Les mémoires* by Philippe de Comines.

Ref: BM; Heredia 3037; Lyell p. 206; NUC; Palau 3856; Salvá 3426.

172. 1587 AGUSTÍN, ANTONIO, ABP. OF TARRAGONA.

Dialogos de medallas, inscriciones y otras antiguedades. Ex bibliotheca Ant. Augustini . . . Tarragona, Felipe Mey, 1587.

Collation: 4°. π², a⁸, b⁶, c-g⁸, h¹⁰, i-k⁸, l⁴, m-o⁸, p⁶, q-r⁸, s⁶, t-v⁸, x⁶, y-z⁸, aa-hh⁸, ii⁴ (b6, f8, h10, l4, p6, z8 and ii4 are cancelled blanks); [2] leaves, 470 pages. [27] leaves of plates. 19.5cm.

Ex-libris of Girardot de Préfond.

Ref: BM; Lyell p. 237; Heredia 3484; NUC; Palau 4097; Salvá 3535.

173. 1588 ARGOTE DE MOLINA, GONZALO.

Nobleza del Andalvzia.. Al catolico don Philipe n.s. rey de las Españas . . . Gonçalo Argote de Molina dedico i ofrecio esta historia . . .Sevilla, Hernando Diaz, 1588.

Collation: f°.⊱⊰⁴,π⁴, 2π², A-Ssss⁴; [10], 348 leaves. 31.5cm.

Contains books 1 and 2 only; books 3 and 4 mentioned in the "Al lector" were never published. Leaves 38 and 39 transposed in binding. Full contemporary blind-stamped calf. Ex-libris of D. P. Rangel.

Ref: BM; Escudero 760; Heredia 3466; NUC; Palau 16170; Palha 4304; Salvá 3540 (contains a map of Jaen which Salvá believes to be integral to the work, yet is not present in any of the copies mentioned above).

174. 1589 HOROZCO Y COVARRUBIAS, JUAN DE.

Emblemas morales de don Ivan de Horozco y Couarruuias . . . Segovia, Juan de la Cuesta, 1589.

Collation: 4°. a-m⁸, n⁶, A-Cc⁸, Dd-Ee⁴, o⁸, Gg-Hh⁸; [101], [9], 104 (i.e. 204), [28] leaves. 20.5cm.

Numerous errors in foliation include leaf 204 misnumbered 104 . "Libro segvndo" and "Libro tercero de las Emblemas morales" each have divisional t.-p. Ex-libris of Edward Gwynn.

Ref: BM; NUC; Palau 116236; Mario Praz. *Studies in Seventeenth-Century Imagery.* 2d. ed. Roma, 1964, p. 374; Salvá 2080.

175. 1589 TOVAR, LUIS.

Libro intitvlado El trivmpho de nvestro señor Iesv Christo . . . nunca hasta agora impresso . . . Compvesto por el bachiller Luys de Tobar . . . Salamanca, Miguel Serrano de Vargas, 1589.

Collation: f°. A⁸, A-R⁸, S²; [8] leaves, 276 pages. 30cm.

Ex-libris of James P. R. Lyell.

Ref: BM; Lyell p. 197-98 and fig. 155; Palau 338297.

176. 1590 . . . *Cronica del serenissimo rey don Iuan segundo* deste nombre. Impressa . . . en la ciudad de Logroño, el año de 1517. Y agora de nvevo impressa . . . Pamplona, Thomas Porralis, [colophon: 20 de marzo] 1590.

Collation: f°. π², *-**⁸, ***⁴, ¶-¶¶⁶, A-Qq⁸, Rr⁶; [34], 317, [1] leaves (last leaf, blank, wanting). 30cm.

For attribution, see above no. 50. Ex-libris of Charles Stuart, baron de Rothesay and of James P. R. Lyell.

Ref: BM; NUC; Palau 64968; Salvá 3119.

177. 1590 ÁLABA Y VIAMONT, DIEGO DE.

El perfeto capitan, instrvido en la disciplina militar, y nueua ciencia de la artilleria. Por don Diego de Alaba y Viamont . . . Madrid, Pedro Madrigal, 1590.

Collation: f°. †⁴, ††-†††⁶ (††† 6 = plate), A-Ii⁸, Kk-Ll⁶; [15], 258, [10, the last blank] leaves, [1] leaf of plates. 30.5cm.

Ref: José Almirante. *Bibliografía militar de España.* Madrid, 1876, p. 9-11; BM (impf.); NUC; Palau 4834; Pérez Pastor, Madrid 319.

178. 1590 [LA MARCHE, OLIVIER DE]

El cavallero determinado, traduzido de lengua francesa en castellana, por don Hernando de Acuña . . . Madrid, Pedro Madrigal, 1590.

Collation: 4°. ¶-¶¶⁴, A-Nn⁴; [8], 112, [2], 27, [3] leaves (last leaf, blank, wanting). 2 copies. 19.5cm.

The full page woodcut illus. by Arnold Nicolaï are from the blocks used in the Antwerp 1553 and 1555 editions. For further details see nos. 157 and 163 (1565 and 1573 editions). Acuña's "Adicional Cavallero determinado" ([2], 27 leaves, with special t.-p.) appears in this edition for the first time.

Copy B: Ex-libris of Sir William Stirling-Maxwell. Title-page and [2] leaves at end wanting, supplied in modern facsimile.

Ref: BM; Brunet III, col. 782; Palau 130354; Peeters-Fontainas p. 191; Peréz Pastor, Madrid 331.

179. 1592 MENDOZA, BERNARDINO DE.

Comentarios de don Bernardino de Mendoça, de lo sucedido en las guerras de los Payses baxos, desde el año de. 1567. hasta el de. 1577 . . . Madrid, Pedro Madrigal, 1592.

Collation: 4°. S-SS⁴, A-Ssss⁴; [8], 336, [12] leaves. 21cm.

Ex-libris of the Biblioteca de Salvá and of Ricardo Heredia.

Ref: BM; Heredia 7046; NUC; Palau 163695; Pérez Pastor, Madrid 387; Salvá 3052.

180. 1598 HERNANDEZ BLASCO, FRANCISCO.

Vniversal redempcion, passion, mverte, y resvrrecion de nuestro redemptor Iesu Christo . . . Compuesto por Francisco Hernandez Blasco . . . segunda impression . . . Toledo, Pedro Rodriguez, 1598.

Collation: 4°. ( )⁴, ¶⁸, A-Bb⁸; [12], 200 leaves. 21cm.

The woodcut illus. on t.-p. and in the text are signed F.H. (i.e. Francisco Hernandez [Blasco]); they are from the same blocks as in the Toledo, 1589 edition. — Cf. Salvá 662.

Ref: BM; Heredia 5482; NUC; Palau 113653, note; Pérez Pastor, Toledo 432.

Portugal

181. 1513 *Este he o liuro z legēda que fala de todolos feytos z payxoões dos sātos martires. em lingoagem portugues. cō apayxō de nosso senhor. assy como ha escreuerō os sanctos quatro euāgelistas. z assy com duas tauoas* . . . [Colophon: Lisboa, João Pedro Bonhomini de Cremona, 17 de agosto de 1513].

Collation: f°. a⁸, b¹⁰, A², 2A⁴, B⁸ (B8 blank), a-q⁸, r⁶, s¹⁰, t-z⁸, &⁸, aa-dd⁸; [32, the last blank], ccxxij, [2] leaves. 32.5cm.

Ex-libris of T. Norton. Leaves signed a3-b10, A1, B3, B5-6 wanting, here supplied in facsimile.

Ref: Anselmo 530; King Manuel 14 and 276; Norton P19.

182. 1514 PORTUGAL. LAWS, STATUTES, ETC., 1495-1521 (EMANUEL I).

Liuro primeiro [-quinto] das ordenações cō sua tauoada q̃ asigna os titulos: z folhas: z tractase nelle dos officios de nossa corte . . . Nouamēte corregido na segūda ēpressam . . . [Colophons: Lisboa, João Pedro Bonhomini de Cremona, 30 de outubro, 15 de dezembro, 11 de março, 24 de março, 28 de junho de 1514].

Collation: f°. 5 pts. in iv. 30.5cm.
Pt. 1: π⁴ (π1 = plate), a-p⁸, q¹⁰; [3], cxxix, [1] leaves, [1] leaf of plates.
Pt. 2: π⁴ (π1 = plate), aa-gg⁸, hh⁶; [3, the last presumably a cancelled blank], lxi, [1] leaves, [1] leaf of plates.
Pt. 3: π⁶ (π1 = plate), aaa-lll⁸; [6, the last presumably a cancelled blank], ij-lxxxviij leaves, [1] leaf of plates.
Pt. 4: A⁴ (a4 = plate), A-F⁸, G⁶; [4], ij-liiij leaves, [1] leaf of plates.
Pt. 5: z⁴, AA-HH⁸, JJ¹⁰; [5], ij-lxxiiij leaves.

Parts 1-5 issued in order 3, 4, 5, 1 and 2. Each part has special t.-p.. T.-p.'s of parts 3 and 4 bear the arms of João II (from the block used in Valentim Fernandes' 1495 edition of *Vita Christi*); t.-p.'s of pts.

5, 1 and 2 bear a new block with arms and sphere of Manuel I within woodcut compartment border; the full-page illus. on verso of the 4th prelim. leaf of pt. 3 (King enthroned within woodcut border) is from the block used in Bonhomini de Cremona's 1513 edition of the *Legēda dos sātos martires.* Full contemporary blind-stamped calf. Two plates (one in pt. 3, the other in pt. 4) wanting. — Cf. King Manuel v.I, p. 255-56, 276 and 280 for description and reproductions.

Ref: Anselmo 532; Barbosa Machado II, p. 733; Brunet IV, col. 206; King Manuel 15; Norton P21; Sousa Viterbo p. 237-38.

183. 1516 LISBON. SANTA CASA DE MISERICORDIA.

O compromisso da confraria de misericordia. [Colophon: Lisboa, Valentim Fernandes & Hermão de Campos, 20 de dezembro de 1516].

Collation: f°. π², a-c⁶; [2] xvij, [1, blank] leaves. 30cm.

Full contemporary vellum portfolio, ties.

Ref: Anne Anninger. "Un oiseau rare, le *Compromisso* de 1516 de Hermão de Campos," *Revista da Biblioteca Nacional*, Lisboa, 1983, 3, (1-2), p. 205-13; William A. Jackson. *Records of a bibliographer; selected papers. Ed. by William H. Bond.* Cambridge, MA., 1967, p. 174 and fig. XIII; Norton P12; not in King Manuel. The following confuse this edition with a close copy probably printed by Germão Galharde ca. 1548: Anselmo 559; Maria M. Cruzeiro. "Obras impressas em Portugal pelo tipógrafo Hermão de Campos (1509-1518), "*Revista da Biblioteca Nacional*, Lisboa, 1981, 1, (1), p. 136-49; Pinto de Mattos p. 165-66; Sousa Viterbo p. 295.

184. 1529 FIGUEIREDO, MARTINHO DE.

Commentu3 in Plinij naturalis historie prologum a iur[is] vtriusq3 doctore Martino Figuereto editū serenissimi portugalie regis senatore. [Colophon: Lisbon, Germão Galharde, June 1529].

Collation: f°. A⁶ (A2 = plate), ✠⁴, a-e⁸, f⁶; [9, the 6th blank], xlv, [1] leaves, [1] leaf of plates. 29cm.

Ex-libris of the Harrach Library and of the Biblioteca Viennensi.

Ref: Anselmo 580 takes his description from the *Catálogo dos reservados,* Coimbra 1032 (impf.); Barbosa Machado III, p. 440; B. Col. III, p. 85-86; BM; King Manuel 24.

185. 1530 FRANCISCANS.

Instituta ordinis beati Francisci. [Colophon: Lisboa, Germão Galharde, 9 de setembro de 1530].

Collation: 4°. a-k⁸, l⁶; lxxxvi leaves. 20.5cm.

In colophon: Nouamēte corregido. The woodcut borders surrounding the illustrations and the capital letters were used by Germão Galharde's predecessors, the printers Valentim Fernandes and João Pedro Bonhomini de Cremona. In Latin and Portuguese. Full contemporary blind-stamped brown calf.

Ref: Anselmo 589; King Manuel 25; Sousa Viterbo p. 123-24.

186. 1537 NUNES, PEDRO.

Tratado da sphera com a Theorica do sol ⁊ da lua. E ho primeiro liuro da Geographia de Claudio Ptolomeo . . . Tirados nouamente de latim en lingoagem pello doutor Pero Nunez . . . E acrecẽtados de muitas annotações ⁊ figuras . . . [Colophon: Lisboa, Germão Galharde, 1 de dezembro de 1537].

Collation: f°. π², a-c⁸, d⁴, aa-bb⁸, cc⁴, A-D⁸, E⁶, F²; [90] leaves. 28cm.

"*Tratado da sphera*" is a translation of Joannes de Sacro Bosco's *Tractatus de sphaera;* "Theorica do sol ⁊ da lua," from Georg von Peurbach's *Theoricae novae planetarum.*

Ref: Anselmo 614; Barbosa Machado III, p. 607; NUC (photostat of the Huntington Library copy); Picatoste 550; Pinto de Mattos p. 425-26; King Manuel 36.

187. 1539 PORTUGAL. CORTES.

Capitolos de cortes. E leys que se sobre alguũs delles fezeram . . . [Lisboa, Germão Galharde, 3 de março de 1539].

Collation: f°. ✠⁴, a-h⁶, i¹⁰, k-l⁸; [4], lxxiiij leaves. 30cm.

Printed on vellum. Title and woodcut illus. on t.-p. within architectural border dated 1534 and signed FD, from the block used in Germão Galharde's 1537 edition of *Constituicoens do arcebispado de Lixboa.* — Cf. King Manuel 35.

Full contemporary blind-stamped brown calf; spine damaged.
Ex-libris of the Cartorci de S. Cruz de Coimbra.

Ref: Anselmo 617, *Catálogo dos reservados,* Coimbra 584, Palha 275, Pinto de Mattos p. 123-24, Sousa Viterbo p. 129, all printed on paper; not in King Manuel.

188. 1514 [i.e. 1539?] PORTUGAL. LAWS, STATUTES, ETC., 1495-1521 (EMANUEL I)

Regimento de como os contadores das comarcas hã de prouer sobre as capellas: ospitaaes: albregarias . . . nouamēte ordenado: ⁊ copillado pello muyto alto ⁊ muyto poderoso rey dom Manuel nosso senhor. E per especial mandado de sua alteza Johã Pedro de bonhomini de Cremona ho mandou empremir . . . [Lisbon, 1514 [i.e. 1539?]].

Collation: f°. a⁶ (a5 = plate), a-f⁸, g¹⁰; [5], lviii leaves, [1] leaf of plates. 28.5cm.

This edition, a faithful reproduction of that of 1514 by Bonhomini de Cremona, was printed by Luiz Rodrigues, whose mark appears on leaf lviiiʳ; it is tentatively dated 1539. — Cf. King Manuel 40 and Sousa Viterbo p. 255. Some of the woodcut borders (fruit, flowers and birds) are from the blocks used in the Paris, 1527 4° edition of Geofroy Tory's *Hore.* Leaf of plates wanting in this copy. Ex-libris of the Livraria de José Maria Nepomuceno.

Ref: Anninger p. 182-83; Silva v.18, p. 164, 242.

189. 1540 ORDEN MILITAR DE SANTIAGO.

Regra ⁊ statutos da ordem de Santiago. [Colophon: Lisboa, Germão Galharde, 24 de setembro de 1540].

Collation: 4°. π⁴ (π2 = plate), A-E⁸, a-e⁸; [3], xl, xxxiiij, [6, the last blank] leaves, 1 leaf of plates. 20cm.

Title within woodcut border (fruit, flowers and birds with, at foot, the crowned L of Louise de Savoie) from the blocks used in the Paris, 1527 4° edition of Geofroy Tory's *Hore.*

Ex-libris of the Livraria de Palha.

Ref: Anninger p. 185 and 187 (plate); Anselmo 623; NUC (this copy only); Palha 2575; Pinto de Mattos p. 481; not in King Manuel (King Manuel 51 describes the 1552 edition of this work, with almost identical t.-p.).

190. 1540 ALVARES, FRANCISCO.

Ho Preste Joam das indias. Verdadera informaçam das terras do Preste Joam, segundo vio ꝫ escreueo ho padre Francisco Aluarez . . . Agora nouamẽte impresso por mandado do dito senhor em casa de Luis Rodriguez liureiro de sua alteza. [Lisboa] [colophon: 22 de outubro de 1540].

Collation: f°. A², B-R⁸, S⁶; [2], 136 (i.e. 128), [6] leaves. 30cm.

Numbers 15-22 omitted in foliation. Ex-libris of James P. R. Lyell.

Ref: Anselmo 1015; BM; Brunet I, col. 204-05 (printed in Coimbra [!]); Giuseppe Fumagalli. *Bibliografia etiopica.* Milano, 1893, 605; HS; King Manuel 42; NUC; Palha 4215; Salvá 3265.

191. 1540 RESENDE, ANDRÉ DE.

L. Andreae Resendii De uerborũ coniugatione commentarius. Lisboa, Luiz Rodrigues [colophon: 1540]. 2 copies.

Collation: 4°. A-P⁴; [60] leaves. 19cm.

Title within architectural border, framed in turn by a woodcut border of fruit, flowers and birds, from the blocks used in the Paris, 1527 4° edition of Geofroy Tory's *Hore.*

Ref: Anninger p. 183 and 184 (plate); Anselmo 1012; BM; King Manuel 43; NUC.

192. 1541 OPORTO, PORTUGAL (DIOCESE)

Cõstituições sinodaes do bispado do Porto ord'nadas pelo . . . sõr dõ Baltasar lĩpo bispo do dicto bp̃ado: ꝫc̃. [Colophon: Oporto, Vasco Diaz Tanco de Frejenal, 1 de março de 1541].

Collation: f°. ✠¹⁰ (✠9 = plate), A-N⁸, O-Q⁶, R⁸, χ¹; [9], cxxx, [1] leaves, [1] leaf of plates. 29cm.

Contains also (each with divisional title): Seguese a ordẽ y modo em que os clerigos sacerdotes desde bispado hã de celebrar as missas. . . . — Seguense os Canones penitenciaes. E casos reservados ao papa. — Seguese a Bulla da Cea do Senhor q̃ se mãdou publicar pollo papa Clemẽte Septimo.

Ref: Anselmo 1073; King Manuel 45; Palha 337; Pinto de Mattos p. 182; Rodriguez Moñino 6.

193. 1542 [SAGREDO, DIEGO DE]

Medidas d'l romano agora nueuamente impressas y añadidas de muchas pieças ꝫ figuras muy necessarias alos officiales que quieren seguir las formaciones delas basas, colunas, capiteles, y otras pieças de los edificios antiguos. [Colophon: Lisboa, Luiz Rodrigues, 15 de enero] 1542.

Collation: 4ᵛ. a-d⁸, e¹²; [44, the last blank] leaves. 21cm.

Author named on [a]1ᵛ.

Ref: Anselmo 1023; BM; NUC; Palau 284924; Picatoste 723; Sousa Viterbo p. 247; not in King Manuel.

194. 1542 OSORIO, JERONYMO.

Hieronymi Osorii lvsitani De nobilitate civili, libri dvo. Eiusdem de nobilitate christiana libri tres. Lisbon, Luiz Rodrigues, 1542.

Collation: 4°. a-p⁸; 120 leaves. 21cm.

In this copy, a cancel slip reading "uirtutis ĩsignia" is pasted over the last two words ("uirtutis ingnia" [!]) of leaf 10ʳ; the catchword on leaf 43ᵛ reads "omnem", leaves 32 and 119 are misnumbered 48 and 108 respectively, and leaves 50 an 56 are correctly numbered. In another Harvard copy, the last two words of leaf 10ʳ read "uirtutis insignia", the catchword of leaf 43ᵛ reads "omuem", leaves 32 and 119 are correctly numbered, and leaves 50 and 56 are misnumbered 54 and 46 respectively.

Ref: Anselmo 1035; BM; Brunet IV, col. 249; Heredia 386; King Manuel 52; NUC; Salvá 3965; Sousa Viterbo p. 248.

195. 1545 FLORANDO DE INGLATERRA. SPANISH.

. . . Comiença la coronica del valiente y esforçado prĩcipe dõ Florãdo d' Inglatierra hijo d'l noble y esforçado prĩcipe Paladiano . . . [Colophon: Lisbona, Germão Galharde, 20 de abril 1545].

Collation: f°. π^2, A-V^8, X-Y^6, a-j^8, k^6; [2], cclj (i.e. ccl) leaves. 30cm.

Number ccxlviij omitted in foliation. In 3 parts; colophon of pt. 2 on leaf clxxij^v dated 20 February 1545. The Condé, Richard Heber copy with the ex-libris of James P. R. Lyell.

Ref: Anselmo 632; BM; King Manuel 58; Sousa Viterbo p. 319-20.

196. 1548 ORDEN MILITAR DE SANTIAGO.

Reegra τ statutos: da ordem de Santiago. [Colophon: Lisboa, 15 de junho de 1548].

Collation: 4°. π^4, a-d^8, e^6, A-D^8, E^{10}; [4], xxxv (i.e. 37), [1], i-xxxviii, [4] leaves. 20cm.

Leaf 37 (1st count) misnumbered xxxv. Printed by Germão Galharde; the illustrations are from the blocks used in his 1540 and 1542 editions. Ex-libris of Thos. Gaisford. T.-p. and [2]nd prelim. leaf reinforced with gauze; lower section of e6 torn and repaired, affecting text and illustration.

Ref: Anselmo 635; BM; King Manuel 63; NUC; Palha 2576; Pinto de Mattos p. 481.

197. 1554 *Coronica do condeestabre d' Portugall*

dom Nuno alurez Pereyra principiador da casa de Bragaça. Sem mudar dãtiguidade de suas palauras nẽ estilo . . . [Colophon: Lisboa, Germão Galharde, 30 de outubro de 1554].

Collation: f°. A-G^8, H^{10}, ✠^{4}; lxvj, [4] leaves. 29cm.

Has been wrongly ascribed to Fernão Lopes. Full contemporary gilt- and blind-tooled green morocco.

Ref: Anselmo 653; Heredia 3235; King Manuel 82; Pinto de Mattos p. 160; Salvá 2898.

198. [1555] THOMAR, PORTUGAL.

Constituyções da jurisdiçam ecclesiastica da villa de Tomar, τ dos mays lugares que, pleno iure, pertençem aa ordem d' nosso senhor Jesu Christo. [Lisbon? 1555].

Collation: f°. ✠^{6}, A-E^6, F^4; [6], xxxii, [2, the last blank] leaves. 29.5cm.

". . . Dada em Lixboa . . . a. xij. dias do mes de janeyro. Anno . . . de. M.D.Lv." on leaf [6]^v. The woodcut initials are printed from blocks owned by

Luiz Rodrigues, later used by Germão Galharde. Ex-libris of the Livraria de Palha.

Ref: Anselmo 656; NUC (this copy only); Palha 343; Silva IX, p. 91, no. 956; not in King Manuel.

199. 1562 CATHOLIC CHURCH. LITURGY AND RITUAL. MISSAL.

Manvale secvndvm ordinẽ almae bracarẽsis ecclesiae. Braga, Antonio de Mariz, July 1562.

Collation: 4°. ✠^{4}, a^6, b^8, c-e^4, f-g^8, h-k^4, l^8, m-n^4, o-p^8, q^6, A^8 (-A6, cancelled blank), B-D^8, E^6, F^8; [8], 3-108 (i.e. 92) leaves, 109-110 pages, 111-150 leaves. 21cm.

Numbers 55 and 92-104 omitted in foliation; leaf [110] was apparently cancelled and the number 110 assigned to the verso of leaf 109 so as not to interrupt foliation.

Ref: Anselmo 837; King Manuel 314; NUC (this copy only); Sousa Viterbo p. 59.

200. 1566 PORTUGAL. LAWS, STATUTES, ETC., 1557-1578 (SEBASTIAN)

Artigos das sisas nouamente emendados per mandado del rei nosso senhor. Lisboa, Manuel João, 1566.

Collation: f°. π^2, A-D^8, E^6, A^8; [2], xxxvij, [1, blank], 7, [1] leaves. 28.5cm.

The privilege (on verso of t.-p.) is granted to Duarte Nunes de Leão. Ex-libris (19th c.) of the Medici family.

Ref: Anselmo 716; BM; King Manuel 337; Palha 271; Pinto de Mattos p. 340; Sousa Viterbo p. 256.

201. 1569 PORTUGAL. LAWS, STATUTES, ETC., 1557-1578 (SEBASTIAN)

Leis extravagantes collegidas e relatadas pelo licenciado Dvarte Nvnez do Liam per mandado do muito alto & muito poderoso rei dom Sebastiam nosso senhor . . . Lisboa, Antonio Gonçalves, 1569.

Collation: f°. ✠^{4}, A-K^8, L^{10}, M-N^8, O^4, P-Y^8, Z^4, AA-BB^8, CC^4, DD-EE^8, FF^4, ✠^{8}, α^8, 2AA^8; [4], 218, [16], 8 leaves. 30cm.

"Annotacões sobre as ordenacões . . ." (8 leaves at end) has special t.-p. In this copy, the blocks of the historiated initials are fairly new; the last line of A1^r reads "cujos despachos ouuessem de passar pela chancellaria, tirando as cartas" and leaf 2AA8r bears the autograph signature of Duarte Nunes de Leão; in another Harvard copy, the text has been entirely reset and the blocks of the historiated initials show signs of wear; the last line of A1r reads "pela chãcellaria, tirãdo as" and the signature of Duarte Nunes on 2AA8r is printed in facsimile. Bound with nos. 202-03 and 206-10 in a volume labeled on spine: Extravagant. de Duarte Nunes de Leam.

Ref: Anselmo 689-90; King Manuel 120; NUC; Palha 273; Sousa Viterbo p. 49.

202. 1578 PORTUGAL. SOVEREIGNS, ETC., 1557-1578 (SEBASTIAN)

Ordenações da nova ordem do ivizo, sobre o abreuiar das demandas, & excuções dellas. Lisboa, Manuel João, 1578.

Collation: f°. A¹⁰; [10] leaves. 30cm.

"Foy pubricada a lei del rey nosso senhor atras escrita . . . per mim Gaspar Maldonado . . . Em Lixboa a xxviij. de ianeiro de M.D. LXXVIII . . .": on A10v. Bound with nos. 201, 203 and 206-10.

Ref: NUC (this copy only); Palha 273; Sousa Viterbo p. 259; not in Anselmo or King Manuel.

203. [1578] PORTUGAL. SOVEREIGNS, ETC., 1557-1578 (SEBASTIAN)

Determinaçois qve se tomaram per mandado del rey nosso senhor, sobre as duuidas que auia antre os prelados, & iustiças ecclesiasticas, & seculares. [Lisboa] Vendese em casa de Iorge Valente liureyro del rey nosso señor. [1578].

Collation: f°. A⁴; [4] leaves. 30cm.

"Foi pubricada a prouisaõ del rey nosso senhor atras escripta . . . per mim Gaspar Maldonado . . . em Lisboa a xvij. de iuuho, de mil & quinhentos & setenta & oyto annos": on A4r. Bound with nos. 201-02 and 206-10.

Ref: Anselmo 1198; King Manuel 387; NUC; Palha 273.

204. 1585 OPORTO, PORTUGAL (DIOCESE)

Constitvições synodaes do bispado do Porto, ordenadas pelo . . . senhor dom frey Marcos de Lisboa bispo do dito bispado. &c. Coimbra, Antonio de Mariz [colophon: 3 de outubro de] 1585. Agora

nouamente acrecentadas com o Estilo da iusticia, & impressas â custa de Giraldo Mendez . . .

Collation: f°. ⊠⁴, ¶⁸, A-R⁸, S¹⁰, A-D⁸; [12], 146, [2], 30 leaves. 27cm.

"Do estyllo, e officiaes da ivstiça do bispado do Porto" ([2], 30 leaves) has special t.-p.

Ref: Anselmo 886; BM; King Manuel 188; NUC; Palha 338; Pinto de Mattos p. 183.

205. 1588 LISBON (ARCHDIOCESE)

Constitvições do arcebispado de Lisboa . . . Agora nouamente impressas . . . Lisboa, Belchior Rodrigues, [colophon at end of pt.3: 15 de maio de] 1588.

Collation: f°. 3pts. in 1v. 26.5cm.
Pt.1: A⁸ (A1 + 1), B-L⁸, M¹⁰; [2], 2-90, [8] leaves.
Pt.2: Aa¹⁰; 10 leaves.
Pt.3: π⁴, A-C⁸, D²; [4], 26 leaves.
Each pt. has special t.-p.

Ref: Anselmo 997; BM; King Manuel 196; NUC; Palha 333; Sousa Viterbo 100.

206. [1590] PORTUGAL. LAWS, STATUTES, ETC., 1580-1598 (PHILIP I)

Ley sobre as sospeiçoens, e embargos. [Lisbon, 1590].

Collation: f°. A⁴; [4] leaves (last leaf, blank, wanting). 30cm.

Caption title. "Foy publicada a ley del rey nosso senhor atras escripta per mi Gaspar Maldonado . . . Em Lisboa a sete dias do mes de iunho de mil, & quinhentos, & nouenta annos . . .": on A3v. Bound with nos. 201-03 and 207-10.

Ref: Anselmo 1228; NUC (this copy only); Palha 273; not in King Manuel.

207. [1591] PORTUGAL. SOVEREIGNS, ETC., 1580-1598 (PHILIP I)

Sobre as confirmaçoes dos padroados e privilegios. &c. [Lisbon, 1591].

Collation: f°. [-]²; [2] leaves. 30cm.

Caption title. "Foy publicada . . . a carta de Sua Magestade atras escrita por mim Gaspar Maldonado . . . Em Lisboa a xxv. de abril de mil & quinhentos

& nouenta & hum annos . . .": on [-]2ʳ. Bound with nos. 201-03, 206 and 208-10.

Ref: Palha 273 repeated by Anselmo 1230; not in King Manuel.

208. [1596] PORTUGAL. SOVEREIGNS, ETC., 1580-1598 (PHILIP I)

Dom Philippe per graça de Deos . . . Faço saber a quantos esta ley virem, que eu fuy informado das desordens, & gastos excessiuos, & despesas que se fazem das rendas dos conselhos das cidades, villas & lugares deste reyno . . . [Lisbon, 1596].

Collation: f°. [-]²; [2] leaves. 30cm.

Title from caption and beginning of text. ". . . El rey nosso senhor, o mandou pello doctor Symão Gonçaluez Preto . . . Dada na cidade de Lisboa, a 13, dagosto de 1596, annos.": on [-]2ᵛ. Bound with nos. 201-03, 206-07 and 209-10.

Ref: Anselmo 1240; King Manuel 408; Palha 273.

209. [1596] PORTUGAL. SOVEREIGNS, ETC., 1580-1598 (PHILIP I)

Provisam, e ley del rey nosso senhor sobre os arcabuzes de menos marca, & gualteyras de rebuço, & adagas estreitas, que cõmummente se chamão de çouella. [Lisboa] Vendese em casa de Iorge Valente liureiro del rey nosso senhor [1596].

Collation: f°. [-]⁴; [4] leaves (last leaf, blank, wanting). 30cm.

Caption title; imprint on leaf [-]3ʳ. "Foy publicada na chancellaria a ley del rey nosso senhor atras escrita per mim Guaspar Maldonado . . . Em Lisboa a sete de nouembro, de mil, & quinhentos, & nouenta & seis annos . . .": on leaf [-]3ʳ. Bound with nos. 201-03, 206-08 and 210.

Ref: Anselmo 1241; King Manuel 409; Palha 273.

210. [1597] PORTUGAL. SOVEREIGNS, ETC., 1580-1598 (PHILIP I)

Provisam pera qve nas cartas, e alvaras, em qve estiuer o sinal de Sua Magestade, senão ponhão registros, nem posses, nem outra cousa algũa, & que em nenhũs autos, nem escripturas, se nomee pessoa algũa por senhor. [Lisboa] Vendese em casa de Iorge Valente, liureiro del rey nosso senhor [1597].

Collation: f°. [-]¹; [1] leaf. 30cm.

Caption title; imprint on verso. "Foy publicada na chancelleria . . . atras escritta per mim Guaspar Maldonado . . . Em Lisboa a quatro de outubro, de mil & quinhentos & nouenta & sete annos": on verso. Bound with nos. 201-03 and 206-09.

Ref: Anselmo 1247; King Manuel 413; Palha 273.

Indices

Index of Authors and Titles

Index of Illustrators

Index of Cities and Printers

References

Aguiló   Aguiló y Fuster, M. Catálogo de obras en lengua catalana impresas desde 1474 hasta 1860. Madrid, 1923.

Alcocer   Alcocer y Martínez, M. Catálogo razonado de obras impresas en Valladolid, 1481-1800. Valladolid, 1926

Anninger   Anninger, A. "Geofroy Tory's borders 'à la moderne' and their later fortunes in Portugal," Essays in honor of James Edward Walsh, Cambridge, [Mass.], 1983, p. 170-95.

Anselmo   Anselmo, A. J. Bibliografia das obras impressas em Portugal no século XVI. Lisboa, 1926.

Antonio, Nov.   Antonio, N. Bibliotheca Hispana nova sive Hispanorum scriptorum qui ab anno MD. ad MDCLXXXIV. floruere notitia. Matriti, 1783-88. 2v.

B. Col.   Biblioteca Colombina. Catálogo de sus libros impresos, publicado . . . bajo la inmediata dirección de su bibliotecario D. Servando Arbolí y Faraudo. Sevilla, Madrid, 1888-1948. 7v.

BM   British Museum. General catalogue of printed books. Photolithographic edition to 1955. London, 1965-66. 263v.

Barbosa Machado   Barbosa Machado, D. Biblioteca Lusitana, histórica, crítica e cronológica. 2a ed. Lisboa, 1930-35. 4v.

Brunet   Brunet, J. C. Manuel du libraire et de l'amateur de livres, 5e éd. originale . . . augmentée d'un tiers par l'auteur. Paris, 1860-65. 6v.

Brunet, Supp.   Brunet, J. C. Manuel du Libraire . . . Supplément par P. Deschamps et G. Brunet. Paris, 1878-90. 2v.

Bullón   Bullón y Fernández, E. Un colaborador de los Reyes Catolicos, el doctor Palacios Rubios y sus obras. Madrid, 1927.

Burger   Burger, K. Die Drucker und Verleger in Spanien und Portugal von 1501-1536, mit chronologischer Folge ihrer Druck- und Verlagswerke. Leipzig, 1913.

Catalina   Catalina García, J. Ensayo de una tipografía complutense. Madrid, 1889.

Catálogo dos reservados, Coimbra   Catalogo dos reservados da Biblioteca Geral da Universidade de Coimbra. (Acta Universitatis Conimbrigensis.) Coimbra, 1970.

Escudero   Escudero y Perosso, F. Tipografía Hispalense. Anales bibliográficos de la ciudad de Sevilla . . . hasta fines del siglo XVIII. Madrid, 1894.

Fernández	Fernández, B. Impresos de Alcalá en la Biblioteca del Escorial, con adiciones y correcciones a la obra Ensayo de una tipografía complutense. Madrid, 1913.
Gallardo	Gallardo, B.J. Ensayo de una biblioteca española de libros raros y curiosos formado con los apuntamientos de B. J. Gallardo, coordinados y aumentados por M. R. Zarco del Valle y J. Sancho Rayon. Madrid, 1863-89. 4v.
Grässe	Grässe, J. G. T. Trésor de livres rares et précieux. Berlin, 1922. 7v. in 8.
Gómez Canedo	Gómez Canedo, L. . . . Las obras de fr. Antonio de Guevara. Madrid, 1946.
Haebler	Haebler, K. Bibliografía ibérica del siglo xv. Enumeración de todos los libros impresos en España y Portugal hasta el año de 1500. La Haya, Leipzig, 1903-17. 2v.
Haebler, Early Printers	Haebler, K. The early printers of Spain and Portugal. London, 1897.
Harrisse	Bibliotheca Americana Vetustissima. A description of works relating to America published between the years 1492 and 1551. [By Henry Harrisse.] New York, 1866.
Hazañas	Hazañas y la Rúa, J. La imprenta en Sevilla. Noticias inéditas de sus impresores desde la introducción del arte tipográfico en esta ciudad hasta el siglo xix. Sevilla, 1945-49. v.1 and 2 only.
Heredia	Catalogue de la bibliothèque de M. Ricardo Heredia, comte de Benahavis. Paris, 1891-94. 4v.
HS	Penney, C. L. List of books printed before 1601 in the library of the Hispanic Society of America. Offset reissue, with additions. New York, 1955.
Huth Library	Huth, H. The Huth Library. A catalogue. London, 1880. 5v.
Huth, Sale	Catalogue of the famous library of printed books, illuminated manuscripts, autograph letters and engravings collected by Henry Huth . . . which will be sold by auction, by Messrs. Sotheby, Wilkinson & Hodge. [London, 1911-20]. 9pts. in 6v.
King Manuel	Manuel II, King of Portugal. Early Portuguese books 1489-1600 in the library of his Majesty the King of Portugal. London, 1929-35. 3v.
Lyell	Lyell, J. P. R. Early book illustration in Spain. London, 1926.
Lyell, Ximenes	Lyell, J. P. R. Cardinal Ximenes . . . With an account of the Complutensian Polyglot Bible. London, 1917.
Madurell & Rubió	Documentos para la historia de la imprenta y librería en Barcelona (1474-1553); recogidos y transcritos por José M.ª Madurell Marimón, anotados por Jorge Rubió y Balaguer. Barcelona, 1955.
Méndez-Hidalgo	Méndez, F. Tipografía española, ó Historia de la introduccion, propagacion y progresos de la imprenta en España . . . 2a ed. corregida y adicionada por D. Dionisio Hidalgo. Madrid, 1861.

Millares Carlo	Millares Carlo, A. Tres estudios bibliográficos. Maracaibo, 1961.
Nagler	Nagler, G. K. Die Monogrammisten. Munich & Leipzig, [1919]. 5v.
Norton	Norton, F. J. A descriptive catalogue of printing in Spain and Portugal, 1501-1520. Cambridge, [1978].
NUC	The National Union Catalogue, pre-1956 imprints. [Chicago], 1968-80. 685v.
Palau	Palau y Dulcet, A. Manual del librero hispano-americano. Barcelona, 1948-77. 28v.
Palha	Catalogue de la bibliothèque de m. Fernando Palha. Lisbonne, 1896. 4pts. in 2v.
Peeters-Fontainas	Peeters-Fontainas, J. "Les éditions espagnoles du 'Chevalier délibéré' d'Olivier de la Marche," *De Gulden passer*, v. 38 (1960) p. 178-192.
Pérez Goyena	Pérez Goyena, A. Ensayo de bibliografía navarra. Pamplona, 1947-64. 9v.
Pérez Pastor, Madrid	Pérez Pastor, C. Bibliografía madrileña de los siglos XVI y XVII. Amsterdam, 1970-71. 3v.
Pérez Pastor, Medina	Pérez Pastor, C. La imprenta en Medina del Campo. Madrid, 1895.
Pérez Pastor, Toledo	Pérez Pastor, C. La imprenta en Toledo . . . desde 1483 hasta nuestros días. Madrid, 1887.
Picatoste	Picatoste y Rodríguez, F. Apuntes para una biblioteca científica española del siglo XVI. Madrid, 1891.
Pinto de Mattos	Pinto de Mattos, R. Manual bibliographico portuguez de livros raros, classicos e curiosos coordenado por Ricardo Pinto de Mattos, revisto e prefaciado pelo snr. Camillo Castello Branco. Porto, 1878
Prescott	Prescott, W. H. History of the reign of Ferdinand and Isabella. Boston, 1838. 3v.
Rodríguez Moñino	Rodríguez Moñino, A. R. Bibliografía de Vasco Díaz Tanco. Valencia, 1947.
Rogent & Durán	Rogent, E. and E. Durán. Bibliografía de les impressions lul·lianes. (Inst. d'Estudis Catalans.) Barcelona, 1927.
Salvá	Salvá y Mallén, P. Catálogo de la Biblioteca de [Vicente] Salvá . . . enriquecido con la descripcion de otras muchas obras de sus ediciones. Valencia, 1872. 2v.
Sánchez	Sánchez, J. M. Bibliografía aragonesa del siglo XVI. Madrid, 1913-14. 2v.
Sanpere	Sanpere y Miquel, S. De la introducción y establecimiento de la imprenta en las coronas de Aragón y Castilla y de los impresores de los incunables catalanes. Barcelona, 1909.
Serrano	Serrano y Morales, J. E. Reseña histórica en forma de diccionario de las imprentas que han existido en Valencia desde la introducción del

arte tipográfico en España hasta el año 1868, con noticias bio-bibliográficas de los principales impresores. Valencia, 1898-99.

Silva Silva, I. F. da. Diccionario bibliographico portuguez. Lisboa, 1858-1923. 22v.

Souhart Souhart, R. Bibliographie générale des ouvrages sur la chasse. Paris, 1886.

Sousa Viterbo Sousa Viterbo, F. de. O movimento tipográfico em Portugal no século XVI. Coimbra, 1924.

Vicaire Vicaire, G. Bibliographie gastronomique. Paris, 1890.

Vindel, Arte Vindel, F. El arte tipográfico en España durante el siglo XV. Madrid, 1949-54. 9v.

Vindel, Escudos Vindel, F. Escudos y marcas de impresores y libreros en España . . . 1485-1850. Barcelona, 1942; Madrid, 1950. 2 pts.

Vindel, Man. Vindel, F. Manual gráfico-descriptivo del bibliófilo hispano-americano (1475-1850). Madrid, 1930-34. 12v.

Front cover: Title-page of Vasco Díaz Tanco de Frejenal's *Libro intitulado Palinodia*. Orense, Printed by the author, 1547.

Tail-piece, p. 74: Printer's mark of Diego de Gumiel, from his edition of Ramón Lull's *Ars inuentiva veritatis*, Valencia, 1515.

Tail-piece, p. 80: Printer's mark of João Pedro Bonhomini de Cremona, from his edition of *Liuro τ legẽda que fala de todolos feytos τ payxoões dos s̃atos martires*, Lisbon, 1513.

Back cover: Printer's mark of Luiz Rodrigues, from his edition of André de Resende's *De uerborũ coniugatione commentarius*, Lisbon, 1540.